# The Struggle For Freedom & Democracy Betrayed

## Memoirs of Miria Matembe as an insider in Museveni's Government

### MIRIA R.K MATEMBE

# THE STRUGGLE FOR FREEDOM
## & DEMOCRACY BETRAYED

ISBN: 9789970524006

P. O. Box 844, Kampala (Uganda)
mrkmatembe@gmail.com

*Layout by:*
*Nahabwe Mark, mackartt1@gmail.com*

■

First Edition

# Dedication

To all those women and men, living or departed, who have committed their lives to struggle for justice, fairness, equality and freedom for the African people.

*He made my mouth like a sharpened sword, in the shadow of his hand he hid me; he made me into a polished arrow and concealed me in his quiver.*

**Isaiah 49:2**

# List of Acronyms & Abbreviations

ACFODE - Action for Development.

CA - Constituent Assembly.

CAD - Constituent Assembly Delegate.

CEWIGO - Centre for Women in Governance.

DP - Democratic Party.

ESO - External Security Organisation.

FDC - Forum for Democratic Change.

FOWODE - Forum for Women in Development.

IG - Inspectorate of Government.

IGG - Inspector General of Government.

ISO - Internal Security Organisation.

ISO - Internal Security Organisation.

KAP - Kalangala Action Plan (of Major Kakooza Mutaale).

KY - Kabaka Yekka.

NAOWO - National Association of Women's Non Governmntal
            Organisations.

NCW - National Council for Women.

NEC - National Executive Committee (of the NRM).

NRA- National Resistance Army.

NRM - National Resistance Movement.

NSARW - National Strategy for Advancement of Rural Women.

PAC - Public Accounts Committee (of the Parliament of Uganda).

PPU - Presidential Protection Unit ( now Special Forces Command, SFC).

PRA - People's Redemption Army.

RDC - Resident District Commissioner.

SDA - Special District Administrator.

UCB -  Uganda Commercial Bank.

UNLA - Uganda National Liberation Army.

UPC - Uganda People's Congress.

UPDF - Uganda People's Defence Forces.

UPM - Uganda Patriotic Movement.

UWESO - Uganda Women's Efforts to Save Orphans.

YWCA - Young Women Christian Association.

# CONTENTS

# FOREWORD

In 1997, I interviewed Hon. Miria Matembe for my book, *When Hens Begin to Crow*. In the book, I remarked that Miria exemplified 'the hen that has begun to crow' and described her as 'a male chauvinist's worst nightmare.' Anyone who has crossed Miria's path and ignored or underestimated her has done so at their peril. Anyone who remotely imagines they can tame her, slow her down, control or manipulate her are in for a rude awakening. Anybody who thinks they can dampen her passion will be greatly disappointed. Miria sums it up very well in these memoirs when she says: 'I am not a project to be managed.' Indeed, Uganda's President Yoweri Kaguta Museveni—celebrating 33 years in office (and counting)—found this out when he appointed her to serve in his Cabinet.

Several factors account for Uganda's current battered democracy. Our history, both pre- and post-independence, is replete with accounts of violent power struggles. Like many other African states, Uganda has been marked by divide-and-rule politics, which its leaders have used to sustain themselves in power. Instruments such as money, promotions, reshuffles, cooptation, ethnicity, language, religion and identity are used to sow dangerous chasms within our communities. To crown it all, very few in our political class are principled enough to turn such inducements down.

But the factors that explain our political situation are not just about the personal. They are mostly structural.

Those factors are created by conditions that extend deep into the socio-economic and political fabric of our society. Systemic, subtle and often invisible to the uncritical eye, those conditions stifle our human agency. They hold us down and prevent us from realizing our greatest ambitions. This is structural violence, namely, the underlying political-economic conditions which hold us hostage to militarism, corruption and abject conditions of poverty. They undermine our ability to control our lives and to transform the status quo. Institutionalized sexism, tribalism, classism, ageism, ablism and so many other isms are all part and parcel of the structural violence that impede democratic processes.

Miria Matembe entered such a political scene in the 1980s when she joined local council politics, eventually becoming a Member of Parliament in the early 1990s. She was an ardent believer in President Museveni's promise for a 'fundamental change' in the wake of Uganda's turbulent politics under Idi Amin and Milton Obote. With her characteristic passion, enthusiasm and religious fervor, Miria lit up Ugandan politics with her demand for equality between men and women, reform of the law, and the ethical reconstruction of the country. It did not take long for Miria to realise that much of what she was fighting against did not belong in the past. That despite the charge that our 'past leaders' had messed up the country, our 'new breed' were not much better. Indeed, we seemed to be walking down the same old political paths of yesteryear. Uganda had not turned a 'new page' nor a 'new chapter,' let alone a new book. It was same old, same old.

In many ways this book represents the deep reflections of profound disillusionment. As an intensely religious individual, it is obvious that Miria is in the confessional. She is candid about her former belief in the system, and the betrayal which the system meted out to her. She confesses to her naiveté about political intrigue, sectarian machination and illegal predatory practices. She is open about her shock and awe at the depths to which her erstwhile comrades were willing to go in the interests of self-aggrandizement and conspicuous consumption. Ultimately, the book is a fascinating exposé of what goes on behind the political scene, a warts-and-all feature of public life in Uganda's contemporary politics. Miria Matembe is every dictator's worst nightmare!

**Sylvia Tamale**
*Professor of Law, Makerere University*

# PREFACE

Born bold, Miria Matembe has grown even bolder. In telling her tale in the pages of this book, she spares no punches. With characteristic courage, she dares throw bare-knuckled blows into every direction: however lofty, however mighty, and however vulnerable that direction may be. Her signature style of speaking is in being bold and blunt. In these pages, both elements are readily manifest. Both are self-confessed by the author herself with repeated references to the ancient biblical prophecy of Isaiah [Chapter 49:1-7]:

*"He gave me a mouth like a sharpened sword...*

*He made me into a sharp arrow..."*

Miria's speechifying is not rooted in fancy figures of speech; delicate degrees of idiom; nor in mellow forms of metaphor; much less in the elastic subtlety of diplomatic discourse. Rather, her speaking talent is embedded in blunt, direct, straight talk; using real words; calling a spade a spade, to leave no possible room for concealing a spade for a more elegant tool. Hers is not the voice of half-hearted ambivalence; not the voice of faint-hearted vagueness; nor, indeed, the voice of crest-fallen repentance-upon-penitence. Hers, rather, is the voice of full-throated clarity; a gallant voice of immense courage and compassion.

The story Miria tells is a cluster of close-knit connections and experiences she shared with people in power: the pilots of politics in her own generation. She was a full-fledged member of the small, intimate coterie of high profile actors perched at the apex of Uganda's political pyramid. Her tale is at once intimate and articulate; laudable and reliable; as well as authentic and authoritative. It gathers together a series of subtle strands of politicking and distils them into a unified summary of Uganda's brand of governance in the present age of the country's history. The tale is as riveting as it is gripping: it is as potent as it is patriotic. Her contribution to an understanding of the contemporary forces at work is immensely invaluable.

Miria's life story, boldly scripted in this tome, is an integral part of Uganda's political history; a finite but telling fragment in the chronicles of our nation's brand of governance. Certainly, Miria Matembe is a molecular particle of that political history. Her personal story orbits pretty close to the nucleus of the centrifugal forces that form the nation's recent history.

From youth to adolescence, right into adulthood, there are no dull or lukewarm moments in Miria's own life narrative. There are only solid episodes of searing passion and fury. The memoirs before you, dear reader, are saturated with the firm and bold voice of a storyteller who is consumed with the passion of her tale—as firm and bold, and as resolute and brave as can be. The decibels of her voice, ringing through these pages, are unmistakable. The candor and the credibility of that voice; plus the deep feeling and the sheer force of that voice, are likewise un-mis-understandable. Hers is the voice of a high energy lady activist.

To say that Miria's voice is loud and voluble, is an understatement. To say that she is credible and laudable is no overstatement. The truth of the matter is that Miria's voice has, over time, been a shrill but lucid voice of missionary commitment to the cause; selfless dedication to the struggle; and total devotion to the mission of promoting and protecting the people's fundamental human rights; fighting impunity; opposing injustice; and accosting gender inequality. The brave tale, bravery told at the frontline of the titanic struggle, is a tale of reverence for the sanctity of the Constitution; and humility under the sacred umbrella of the Rule of Law.

The tapestry of Miria's life is woven in the fabric of a cause—a noble cause of humanity's inalienable rights; the liberty of the citizenry; the equality of the two genders, and the fraternity of the whole. It is to this cause that Miria has dedicated her time, devoted her life, and consecrated her soul. With characteristic energy and bravery, Miria has raised her voice [both verbally and in print] to attack tyranny, assault injustice, and combat corruption where-so-ever, when-so-ever, and how-so-ever these three vices have reared their dread head. In this book, Miria the warrior does so with clarity and dexterity verging on the sacrificial, if not the suicidal! For her bravery and gallantry we, the people, owe her a delightful debt of fraternal salutations. For her perseverance and resilience to the cause of a more humane society, the ation is much the richer.

The extraordinary courage and the singular clarity of her voice, bespeak the candor of the heart; not the cryptic obscurity of the head. It bespeaks the open-handed profundity of her feelings; not the sinister close-fisted animosity of sedition or subversion. The story she tells is a cry of lamentation for the fatherland; not a call to rebellion against the motherland. Yes, the audacity of her voice bursts like a blast of outraged wind ringing in the readers' ear, bearing awesome energy of intense emotion but, an emotion that bears no malice; that carries no treachery; much less the clandestine duplicity of an underhand conspirator.

All too evident in her lamentation, is a palpable hunger for the transformation of her country's politics; and an unquenchable thirst for the transfiguration of her nation's governance. Beneath and behind her relentless screaming in this book, Miria is crying her heart out; grieving for and craving the noblest possible motivation: to bring a catharsis to a nation hurting on the inside; to bring closure and healing to a country whose nerves have been on edge for the last half century. She seeks not to harden, but to unify the divisions that run across the fault lines of our society. She seeks not to pry open the wounds that afflict us as a people, but to soothe and to heal them: to set us at peace at last!

Miria's story is a story of three passions: passion for cause; passion for public service; and passion for the divine. The tripartite mixture of passion, politics and proclamation of her faith in the divine providence is indisputable. The passion for the cause is unmistakable. The politics driving the passion is undeniable. The spirituality overshadowing the twain is unalterable. The story would be incomplete without a recognition and appreciation of those threefold passions. Like a set of triplets, the trilogy of Miria's passions oozes and flows in unison—each part enriching the other parts; all edifying the whole.

May the elusive bell of liberty and the muffled trumpet of justice ring loud and proud in our country, in our time!

Enjoy the reading. Tickle the senses. Nourish the mind. Edify the soul!

**James Ogoola**
*Canon of the Church;*
*Chairman, The Elders Forum of Uganda;*
*Emeritus Principal Judge of Uganda.*

# ACKNOWLEDGMENT

*"Lord, you have assigned me my portion and my cup. You have made my lot secure. The boundary lines have fallen for me in pleasant places surely I have a delightful inheritance."* **Psalms 16: 5-6**

First and foremost, I want to thank God, the God of heaven and earth who created me and made me the person that I am; a woman of purpose and destiny. I am so grateful that He enabled me to realize my childhood dream, which originated from my lived experience of discrimination, inequality and injustices against women and girls. My life purpose to fight against this inequality, injustice and discrimination was cut out for me at the age of nine years, way back in the early 1960s as I lived in my birth village of Rutooma, in Kashari County, Mbarara District in western Uganda.

Not only did God give me favour to realize this childhood dream, but He also enabled me to document the experience of my struggles in my first publication, *"MIRIA MATEMBE: Gender Politics and Constitution Making in Uganda, 2002."* Now that He has once again blessed me with yet another publication on my struggles for democracy and good governance for my country Uganda, I am short of words to show my gratitude to God, but only to praise His name forever.

I wish to express my gratitude to Tech-Write Consults Ltd, in particular Benjamin Mpaka, the lead researcher who worked so tirelessly to ensure that finally my second dream hatched in my heart in 2006 becomes a reality. I started on this book in 2006 after quitting elective politics. So this project has taken me over a decade to complete and I believe that it would have taken another decade if Benjamin had not come on board. But more importantly I must thank the Ford Foundation Nairobi Office through Mr. Maurice Makoolo who found my proposal for this book a worthy cause and supported it financially. This enabled me to engage Tech-Write Consult Ltd to assist me finish the pet project.

Several times when I experienced the writers' block and enthusiasm failed me in the course of writing this book, I thought that probably it wasn't God's will that I go ahead with it. I would then put it aside and pray. Then once again the enthusiasm would re-surface and I would have the passion to begin again. It was in this process that I was introduced to Tech-Write Consult Ltd and thereafter the game changed and the result is this book. Benjamin, I want you to know that I am so grateful for all your efforts, your encouragement and determination to ensure that we got this work out to the world. May you be blessed and excel in your endeavors to make your organization successful.

Special thanks go to both Prof. Sabiti Makara and Doreen Baingana for their great input in editing the manuscript. Doreen, being a writer herself, went an extra mile to ensure that the publication meets the acceptable standard. While I was still not so sure that I should indeed publish this work, Prof. Makara's comments motivated me so much to publish this book. I am indeed grateful to you my brother and sister.

I am so thankful to His Lordship Justice James Ogoola, the former Principal Judge of Uganda, for honoring me by writing the wonderful introduction to this book. I was so humbled and excited when he immediately, without any hesitation, gave a positive answer to my humble request. Thank you my Lord for sticking to our cause for justice and integrity.

My dear sister Sylvia Tamale, although I was very sure that you would indeed accept my request to write a foreword to this book, I do not take you for granted. I am very grateful to you. You and I are sisters in the struggle forever despite our spiritual differences, a lesson for all feminists and other strugglists that we do not have to believe or act the same so as to struggle together for the cause of equality and justice.

To my beautiful family, I want you to know that I have had tremendous joy and great value added to my life because of having you as part of me. I am so grateful to all of you my children not only my biological sons and daughters-in-love but also special nieces, nephews and other special daughters that I have had the joy of mothering.

My sweet caring Alice (RIP) and your husband Prof. William Bazeyo, my dynamite loving Anna and your husband Peace Taremwa, my ever smiling and calm model Maude with your husband Bruce Kanabahita; and my little soft-spoken Frankline, you are indeed the treasures of my heart. Without you life could not have been what it is today.

To my special God-given daughters; Faith (RIP) and your husband Tom Oluka, my brilliant, intelligent little

Rachael Okuja, my sharp marketer Cathy Zalwango and soft, simple-hearted but determined Mercy Atuhebwe. May you be blessed for bringing special joy to my heart. The joy of nurturing and making a difference in your lives for which God has been rewarding me is immense.

To my very own Godwin, Gideon, Gilbert and Grace, my sweet daughters-in-love, Tyna, Rachael and Naome, what can I say? Your love, understanding, encouragement, appreciation and tolerance of my tough love for you, have all given me the meaningful and fulfilled life that I now enjoy in the evening of my life. I pray that each one of you lives to be a great man or woman of destiny to God's glory. Thank you for giving me a third generation in my cute grandchildren. Of course Maude and Bruce, you are even more special for making me a grandmother of twins.

To the special man in my life, Nicky, you certainly know how much I value you, especially for the gift of the total freedom I enjoy in this equal partnership of our marriage. Indeed I can only say that God, having cut out the purpose for my life that required freedom of thinking, mobility and action, He gave you to me as my life partner. Sincerely, Nicky, you are an extremely rare Munyankole man and I cannot find words that are appropriate enough to express my gratitude to you. I highly value your total support for me and love for all my women colleagues in the women's movement, not forgetting your love for, and participation in the struggle itself. Honestly without a husband of your personality and character by my side, I would never have been the woman that I am today. May the good Lord reward you immeasurably.

Finally, may I thank His Excellency President Yoweri Museveni, the president of Uganda for now more than thirty years, for appointing me to his cabinet as Minister of Ethics and Integrity, a position I held for nearly five years. Without this appointment I would never have been close enough to write this book as an insider who saw and experienced what is documented in this book. I sincerely wish him a peaceful retirement and a happy life thereafter.

May all of you be blessed as you read the work of my hands.

**Miria Matembe**

## Chapter One

# From Pharaoh to 'Free-doom'

### Early Childhood and the Big Dream – I Want to be a *Pleader*

“ You are useless. That is why you have failed to manage your home. No wonder your husband has chased you away. You useless woman,” I heard the unmistakable angry voice of my father. “Go back to your husband. Go back.”

“I don't want to go back. I can't go back to that good-for-nothing man. I am not a drum to be beaten like that,” my aunt pitifully replied.

"A man is a man. Let him have his way. But tomorrow you must pack up and go back to your home, you useless sister of mine," my father insisted.

"I am not useless! My bride price was paid in full. I brought cows to this home. I have produced sons for that man. I am not useless," my aunt cried out.

Growing up in rural Kashari in Mbarara district, I witnessed many harrowing incidents of the mistreatment of women at the hands of men but this particular incident hurt me the most. It is still fresh and vivid in my memory. Here was my poor aunt married to what I would call a vagabond drunkard man, who used to go away from home for a long time, presumably to work as a casual labourer somewhere far away, while my aunt stayed at home and fended for herself and the children. After some months, my aunt's husband would return home with nothing; neither money nor clothes for his children and wife. Instead of thanking her for keeping the home and children well, he would beat and mistreat her. But when she sought refuge at our home, my father – her own brother – did not show any sympathy for his sister. Instead, he took the side of the vagabond drunk!

Such injustice against women and girls did not sit well with me. In my young mind arose a strong feeling of resentment. I thought: "But why must it always be like this for women? Why?" I then came to learn that in my community, women were not as important as men because they were deemed as inferior.

Even in those early formative years, this was not acceptable to me. When I was about nine years old, I came to know that when people are accused of committing crimes they engage 'pleaders' to plead for them. On asking around who this pleader person was, I was told that he was a lawyer. And just like that, my career goal and ambition was set. I wanted to become a pleader – a pleader for women. It was the only way to help women and girls fight against injustices and discrimination. So by the time I joined secondary school I had made up my mind that I would study law and become a *pleader*.

Not only did I witness the scourge of gender inequality, I personally experienced it. I know how it feels and how it hurts to be unjustly treated because one is a girl or woman. I often had to miss class to stay home and help with household chores. Sometimes I missed school due to late payment of my fees and yet my brother's fees were always paid on time because he was a boy and therefore he never missed any classes. Despite that, I was a brilliant student and did not repeat a single class. Although I was the fourth born among my siblings, I became the first member of my family to be admitted to a secondary school.

While in Senior Two at Bweranyangi Girls Senior Secondary School, my brother Sam, who had repeated some classes, finally gained admission to secondary school as well. Unfortunately, my parents could not afford to pay secondary school fees for both of us, and so they opted to withdraw me from school and send me to a Primary Teacher Training Institute where education was free, and pay for my brother – just because he was a boy. Can you imagine!

You can picture my shock and disappointment when one day the headmistress, Ms Hall, called me to her office and, in the presence of my mother, broke the sad news to me that my mother had come to withdraw me from school to take me to Bishop Stuart Teacher Training College, Kakoba. This news cut through my heart like a knife and tears started flowing down my cheeks. I let out a very loud, "NO!"

Ms Hall seemed empathetic, but I was disappointed that even though she knew how bright and driven I was, she did not fight for me. "I am very sorry, my dear, but you should have pity on your parents," she said. "They cannot afford school fees for both of you. What do you want them to do?"

I felt betrayed by Ms Hall. I expected her to defend me and my right to education as a girl, especially since Bweranyangi was a girls' only school. I did not expect her to support my parents who were sidelining a girl in favour of a boy! For me, this was the height of injustice. Moreover, it would have been the death of my dream of becoming a pleader, so I had to resist it by all means possible.

I quickly thought of a solution to my plight. "But Ms Hall, I have heard that the government gives bursaries to bright students whose parents can't afford school fees. Can't I get a bursary? Where do they give out the bursaries?"

She replied that we could try the Education Officer at the Mbarara District headquarters. I quickly got up and asked my mother whether she knew the Education

Officer's office.

"My daughter," said mother, "I know where the District headquarters is, but I do not speak English. How shall we ask for the school fees?"

"Quick, mother, let's go," I urged, "leave the English and the talking to me."

From Bweranyangi, in the present-day Bushenyi District, mother and I traveled to Mbarara in pursuit of the District Education Officer. Soon we were seated outside the District Education Office, watching people going in and out, but we were clueless on whether to knock or just barge in. Luckily, the District Education Officer came out of his office to go to lunch. Holding my mother's hand, and motioning her to get up, I sprang up and stood in front of the District Education Officer.

"How can I help you, young lady?" asked the officer.

"Sir, I want school fees," I replied, and I burst out crying. He invited us to his office. We entered and sat down. Amidst sobs, I explained my predicament while the officer listened attentively. I could see that he was moved by my passion for education.

"Sorry, stop crying. It will be alright," said the officer. "Go back to school and we shall see what can be done about your school fees. What is your name?"

"Koburunga," I replied. "Miria Koburunga."

Within a week's time, my agony turned into excitement. Ms Hall summoned me to her office again; this time to give me the good news that I had received a bursary to cover my school fees for the entire O Level period.

So, I, at the tender age of 14, managed to secure myself a bursary for my school fees. I learnt that if you resist, take action, stay firm, and with God on your side, you will get what you want. That is how I got my bursary. People talk of the National Resistance Movement, but resistance in me started long ago: the urge to resist discrimination, unfairness and injustice towards women and girls.

After successfully finishing my O Level, I joined Namasagali College for Advanced Certificate of Education (A Level). Even though I had been a member of the Debating Society while at Bweranyangi, it was at Namasagali College that I honed my craft as a public speaker. Among the high school subjects I studied was European history, where we learnt about parliamentary debates in the British House of Commons. I enjoyed those parliamentary debates so much that I started imitating the style of the British members of parliament during our school debates. That was when the idea of becoming a parliamentarian was hatched. My vision of becoming a lawyer was now getting enlarged, having learnt that laws were debated and enacted by parliament.

I now wanted to study law to see what it provided for in relation to the discrimination and injustices against women. In case it was inadequate in providing for women, I would then, besides pleading for them, become an MP so as to make appropriate laws for the empowerment of women. Therefore, from the onset, I did not aspire to become an MP for self-aggrandizement or prestige. I dreamt of securing a platform to espouse the cause for gender equality and women's empowerment by pleading for women and enacting laws that would be sensitive and responsive to the needs, interests and concerns of women.

After passing my A Level exams, I was admitted to Makerere University to study Law, amid relentless protests from my father that girls are only good for nursing or teaching.

## My Life at Makerere University

All along I had witnessed many injustices visited upon me, my family members and the community at large. However, it was at Makerere University that I got exposed to national politics. As a law student, I was, of course, eager to follow what transpired in politics both at the university and at the national level.

When I joined Makerere, Olara Otunnu was the Guild President. In this position, Otunnu was a powerful and key player in national politics, especially in his vehement opposition and condemnation of Amin's politics. Comrade Otunnu, as he was fondly called, was a tough, fearless, intelligent, controversial and celebrated leader whose life and views were regularly reported in the university bulletin. In those days, students who ascended to guild presidency were charismatic and brilliant individuals who usually went on to become national leaders. In my opinion, he was the last most powerful and influential Guild President that Makerere University has ever had.

The times were very bad, of course, with the 'disappearance' of the regime's real and perceived enemies.

In the midst of that, we learnt that Comrade Otunnu had run away into exile to evade capture by Amin's henchmen because of his forthright opposition to his government. A story was told that some of the students who were in Amin's intelligence team leaked the plot to Otunnu and he had to jump through a window of one of the University's halls of residence to escape into exile in 1973. In the wake of Otunnu's escape, Amin banned the use of the title 'President'. All clubs, guilds and societies such as the Rotary Club that previously used the title 'President' had to change to the use of 'Chairman'. Idi Amin effectively became the only person entitled to use the title 'President'.

I was at that time not very interested in participating in politics, but I contested against Specioza Wandira *(who later became Dr Specioza Wandira Kazibwe)* for chairperson of Mary Stuart Hall of residence and lost.

In those days, Makerere was the heartbeat of the politics of the country. Students and lecturers alike came out to strongly condemn the bad politics of the day. In one such demonstration against the dictatorship of Idi Amin, a student called Sserwanga, who was actually a person with a disability, was shot and killed at the small gate near University Hall that led out to Wandegeya trading centre. I remember that day vividly because I was personally affected as Sserwanga was my classmate. That particular day, a Tuesday, came to be known as 'Black Tuesday'. On the subsequent Tuesdays, many students dressed in black to mourn and commemorate the cold blooded murder of our fellow student. Therefore, the recent concept of civil society's 'Black Monday' or Forum for Democratic

Change's (FDC) 'Black Tuesday' is not new. These are time-tested acts of civil disobedience against the excesses of the State.

While at Makerere, I had a very personal encounter with the injustices against women. After receiving my student allowance, which we called 'boom', I went to town to shop for a few clothes because I also wanted to dress like a modern university girl. I bought a pair of very elegant and stylish bell-bottom trousers. I got to my room and tried them on once more. They were a perfect fit. I could not wait to wear them. Alas, that was not to be! That very evening, Idi Amin put out the decree that banned women from wearing trousers and mini-skirts or mini-dresses. I sat down, cried, mourning for my bell-bottom trousers that were never going to see the light of day. To the amusement of my roommate, Monica Mirembe, every visitor to my room had to hear the sad story of my new trousers; I simply could not get over it. Eventually, I got a tailor to cut the trousers into a skirt, but still, it never gave me the gratification of my elegant bell-bottom trousers. What business did the State have in choosing what I wore?

The 1973 decree to ban mini-skirts, wigs and trousers was on the basis that they presented a threat to public morality and on grounds of anti-colonialism and anti-westernisation. The ban on trousers was later to be lifted when Amin learnt that they were a style of clothing worn by women in some of the Muslim countries he held in awe.

Another personal encounter with the wrath of Amin's draconian rules was when I was arrested for wearing a short dress. It was at the end of my first year at the university. I was traveling back home for my holidays. Upon reaching the Mbarara bus park, I was stopped and arrested. I was forced into a vehicle by one Inspector Kigozi, and driven to the area of Rubaya in Kashaari. Luckily for me, there were some other men in the vehicle who had been arrested too. I, believe, that is how I survived the worst. In the circumstances of the time, that so-called inspector could have raped me.

At around 3:00 p.m., the man drove us to Mbarara police station. Upon arrival at the station, I was ordered to remove my shoes and enter the cells. As a law student, I of course knew my rights. I protested and refused. First of all, my dress was not too short because it wasn't two inches above the knee line or higher, as per the decree. Inspector Kigozi threatened to beat me and I made a loud alarm as I dashed to the office of the Superintendent of Police, who happened to be my uncle called Ephraim Rwakanengyere. My uncle was surprised and furious to see me in that state. He reprimanded Inspector Kigozi. That is how I narrowly survived what could have been my worst nightmare. Once you got into those cells, anything could happen.

Long after this incident, I met my future husband, Nekemia Matembe. We got married at the end of my second year. That is how I acquired the Matembe name. Everybody now knows me by the name, Miria Matembe.

## Unjust Legal Regime for Women and Idi Amin's Reign of Terror

Studying Law at Makerere opened my eyes to the manner in which gender inequality had over the years been systematically entrenched into the laws and systems of Uganda. The law was not only discriminatory against women, it was also extremely inadequate in providing for and protecting them. This was during Idi Amin's oppressive regime. Some of the worst cases of injustice against women were being perpetuated by the Head of State himself and his close henchmen. Amin's administration put out one decree after another, many of which were obviously targeted at undermining the status of women. Some extremely draconian and absurd ones included: the decree that banned women from wearing mini-skirts, trousers and wigs, as mentioned earlier; and another decree that legitimised polygamy. Life for women was extremely sad. Many women were widowed in their 20s. Their husbands were either killed or made to 'disappear'.

It was during those bad times that I graduated with an Honours degree in Law in 1976. Finally, I had achieved my childhood dream. I was now a lawyer - a pleader. I felt I was ready to take on the world and advocate for just laws.

However, my big achievement was choked by the general state of hopelessness that prevailed in the country then. Amin had established military rule and abolished parliament. Therefore, the second part of my dream was thrown into abeyance. As if that was not frustrating enough, I could not even carry out my first objective of pleading for women. The political environment of military dictatorship was so bad that there was no way I could come out to call for and defend women's rights when everybody's human rights were being violated with impunity and brutality.

I do not want to say that my law degree was a Pyrrhic victory. However, the truth is that the then prevailing political environment shook my resolve. I had single-mindedly pursued my dream of becoming a lawyer. I had grand dreams of getting a platform to mobilise women and talk to them about the need to liberate ourselves from all the injustices meted out to us. I envisioned myself standing like Jesus giving His Sermon on the Mount of Beatitudes, calling upon women to rise and join me in the struggle. But, alas, that was not to be.

By the end of my law course, Amin had by decree banned women's non-governmental organisations. He passed the decree in 1978 establishing the National Council for Women (NCW), while at the same time banning other organisations including NGOs, Mothers' Union and the YWCA. Article Number 4 of the decree states: "For avoidance of doubt, it is declared that with effect from the commencement of this decree, no women's organisation shall continue to exist, or be formed except in accordance with this decree". Essentially, this ban left no free machinery by which women could organize, mobilise or even, meet and network. The situation was less than ideal, but I resolved not to despair. In my mind, my dream of championing the women's cause was not shattered; it was only a dream deferred. As a woman of faith, I prayed and believed that the opportune time would soon come.

All I could do after graduation was to look for a job. I was burning with the desire to fight injustice so I joined the Ministry of Justice where I was attached to the Directorate of Public Prosecutions (DPP). This is a department responsible for the investigation and prosecution of criminal offenders. There I thought I could play a bit of that role, and generally do my small part in building the nation. But I was in for a rude awakening!

During my brief stay at the DPP, I was deeply frustrated by the wanton injustice that was going on in a place that was supposed to execute justice. Poor, miserable petty offenders involved in small offences like stealing a chicken, or brewing crude *waragi*, would be arrested and imprisoned for so long, and could not be released on bail for lack of money and people to stand surety for them. Yet big time criminals involved in crimes like robbery were released on bail because they had money and people to stand surety for them. Seeing those miserable petty offenders go back to prison every time their cases came for mention was heart wrenching.

I resolved not to be party to this injustice. I quit the job within about four months of my employment. I joined the Uganda College of Commerce (present day Makerere University Business School), as a lecturer in law. I stayed there for hardly two years before Idi Amin was overthrown by the Uganda National Liberation Front (UNLF) in 1979.

## Post-Amin Upheavals

In the true unshakable spirit of Ugandans, mammoth crowds lined the streets to celebrate the fall of Amin. The UNLF soldiers and their Tanzanian *bakombozi* counterparts were hoisted high as heroes. Again, there was a huge sense of optimism. "Surely, after Amin, things can only get better," thought many Ugandans, myself included.

Unfortunately, our excitement and sense of optimism was very short lived. Between the time of Amin's ouster and Obote II, there were several heads of state, some at the helm for just a few months. The feel-good factor that had brought smiles to many Ugandans' faces steadily faded as life got worse.

Within that short period between 1979 and 1980, before the widely-acknowledged-as-rigged general elections of December 1980 which brought in the Obote II government, power changed hands like cards in a poker game: from President Lule to President Binaisa; from Binaisa to Muwanga and the Military Commission; and from Muwanga to Obote. Life in that short period of time was extremely uncertain.

I remember a wave of gruesome murders that took place that up to now, have not been fully solved. These murders were committed in homes in a pattern that suggested that they were related plots of some sort.

There was the shocking murder of Colonel Ruhinda of Igara who was killed while visiting George Kihuguru's home at Makerere University. Colonel Ruhinda had been one of the heroes of the UNLF that had removed Amin. Then there was the murder of a distinguished surveyor from Toro called Katuramu Kaija, followed by the murder of a banker called Bagonza, and thereafter the murder of Patrick Bakuru of the Ministry of Lands. Bakuru's wife, Faith, who was a former schoolmate of mine, was shot at but narrowly managed to survive.

We came to learn, by way of rumour, that this was a plot by one of the many returnees from exile, whose grudge with these three distinguished men was over a house that the returnee had mortgaged to a bank before he ran into exile. Word was that when the owner of the house returned to Uganda, he found that his house had been sold. Of course, it had been sold since he had not been paying his mortgage. The three victims had to pay with their lives for executing their duties.

I understand Katuramu had valued the house, Bagonza who worked with the bank where the house had been mortgaged had sold the house, while poor Bakuru, being a Registrar in the Ministry of Lands, had transferred the house to the new buyer. I never got to know who the buyer was and I do not know whether he survived the murderous spree.

The Head of the Baha'i faith in Africa, Mr Olinga, his wife and three children were also murdered at their home. I personally attended the funeral of the Olingas at the Baha'i Temple in Kampala. It was so tragic and traumatizing. The only surviving children were those who were out of the country at the time, including George Olinga, who now lives in Uganda.

This was followed by the murder of other professionals especially doctors, including Dr Obacha, Dr Jack Barlow, Dr Kamulegeya and Dr Bagenda. It is so strange that up to now, we have never known the real reasons for all these ghastly murders of such eminent Ugandans.

Life was so tense and uncertain. We went to sleep wondering who we would find murdered the next day – such was the short-lived jubilation of the 1979 liberation war. All those wanton murders pointed to a failed state: a government administration that was failing in its cardinal duty of protecting the lives and properties of Ugandans.

It was in the midst of this extremely unpleasant environment that Dr Apollo Milton Obote returned from Tanzania, where he had lived in exile for nine years, to run for the presidency of Uganda for the second time.

At around that time, a new party entered into the fray of Uganda's politics. The Uganda Patriotic Movement (UPM) was formed under the leadership of a young and charismatic Mr Yoweri Museveni, to contest in the 1980 elections. The real battle, however, was between the two antagonistic traditional parties – Uganda People's Congress (UPC) and the Democratic Party (DP). In the highly electric presidential elections of 1980, UPC's flag bearer was Obote while the DP's candidate was Dr Paulo Kawanga Ssemogerere.

With the return of the country to multiparty politics, I chose to join Museveni's UPM. My choice was really simple. I could not join the traditional parties because they were largely based on tribal and religious affiliations. The charisma of the young and progressive Museveni easily won over many of us young people.

Indeed, the new wave of excitement got many young people dreaming big. My brother-in-law, Ambrose Rwomwiju had decided to contest for the Ibanda District seat under UPM, but unfortunately his bid was cut short when he died in a car accident on a trip to Ibanda for consultations. At that time I was expecting a baby, and when I traveled on those bad roads for the funeral, I nearly had a miscarriage and had to be put on bed rest for the rest of the pregnancy. So, being bed-ridden, I was neither able to actively campaign nor cast my vote for UPM.

I could not join UPC for two other reasons. Back in 1966, Obote had abrogated the national constitution, and as a lawyer, that act did not augur well with me. Besides, he was so resented in Buganda and I thought that even if he won the presidency, there would be no peace in Buganda because the Baganda would simply not accept him. This, in fact, eventually came to pass.

The third reason why I did not join UPC was my personal resentment and dislike of its leader. In his first regime, Obote had imprisoned five of his ministers, including Hon Grace Ibingira who came from my home village. Grace Ibingira was our role model as children. We grew up looking up to him for inspiration, while our parents in Rutooma village cherished and loved him so much. His imprisonment shortly after independence, together with my cousin, Captain Levis Mugarura, both from Rutooma-Bwizibwera, Kashaari, did not please us at all.

Therefore, when Obote returned, we were worried that he would come after their lives. Amin had released them from prison and they had been living in the country as free citizens. True to our premonition, Levis 'disappeared' – was most likely murdered – immediately after the 1980 general elections, and his body has never been found, while Hon Grace Ibingira had to flee into exile, again.

The electoral process was extremely violent and elections were, to many accounts, rigged in favour of Obote and his UPC. During the campaigns, Museveni had declared that he would go 'to the bush' to fight to overthrow the government if the elections were rigged. True to his word, in February 1981, alongside 40 comrades, with only 27 of them armed, Museveni attacked Kabamba military barracks and launched a protracted guerrilla war against the Obote II government.

## Obote II and Museveni's NRA Guerrilla War

With the controversy surrounding Obote's second stint in power, the unfortunate repetitive cycle of violence was predictable. Against the backdrop of a heavily rigged and violent election, there was widespread anger and frustration among many Ugandans. And it appeared that the UPC government set out in full force to persecute both its real and imaginary enemies.

I continued teaching at UCC, Nakawa, even as I was harassed by the Principal, Mr Ben Owani, who became extremely resentful of the Banyankore. Whenever he met one of us on the college campus, be it a lecturer or a student, whether it was in class or on the compound, he reminded us that our place was in 'the bush' and that we should go and join our brother Museveni in the bush where we belonged. He would say, "Look at your nose; what do you think you are doing here? Don't you know where you belong?" He made our stay at the college so miserable and unbearable that actually some of the students abandoned their studies and went to the bush.

At that time, the NRA war in the Luweero triangle was raging. On one side, the rebels led by Museveni were determined to liberate the country, while on the other side a bullish Obote threatened to exterminate Museveni and his 'bandits'.

Mr Owani's harassment became too unbearable for me and so in 1982, I left UCC and got a job at Bank of Uganda as a lecturer seconded to the Uganda Chartered Institute of Bankers, Kampala, where I worked up to 1989.

## A New Wave of Optimism under Museveni and the NRM

After five years of the NRA war that raged mainly in the Luweero triangle of Buganda, Museveni took over power in 1986 from the short-lived Tito Okello Lutwa's regime that had overthrown Obote in July, 1985. The rag-tag army was, in typical Ugandan fashion, welcomed on the streets of Kampala by jubilating crowds. Again, Ugandans dreamt of bright times ahead.

"Surely, this cannot be another false dawn," I thought to myself. I was challenged by the young officers of the

NRA who had actively taken part in the struggle. These were young people in my age bracket who had sacrificed their lives for the liberation of the country. My uncle, Hon Major John Kazoora, who became the Special District Administrator for Kampala, was a big influence on me at that time. Whenever I looked at him and his friend Major Victor Bwana, I was challenged and inspired, and sensed that the time was nigh for me to reawaken my dream. I felt that the environment was getting conducive enough for me to embark on my mission: the struggle for women's rights.

Museveni's government came with a new momentum and it placed 'the woman question' high on the agenda. The NRM introduced a number of affirmative action interventions to uplift the status of women, including the creation of a special seat of Secretary for Women Affairs on the Resistance Committees and Councils (now called Local Councils – LCs).

This was a dream come true for me. The much awaited platform from which to mobilise women was finally before me, courtesy of the good policies and conducive socio-political environment offered by the new government. I did not waste any time embracing Museveni's government. This was the decisive moment to usher me into my dream – a critical turning point in my life. I felt reinvigorated and my dreams became alive again. This was it. My life would never be the same again!

I quickly embraced the available opportunities by joining the Resistance Committees and Councils (RC) right from the bottom – my village in Port Bell, Luzira, up through to the RC V in Kampala District. At the district level, I became the Secretary for Mass Mobilization and Education. In this position, I was unstoppable. I traversed all the divisions of Kampala, mostly on foot, preaching the message of the NRM's 10 Point Program and gender equality. The sheer enthusiasm, commitment and purpose with which I descended onto the public scene could not go unnoticed.

It was not long before I started attracting media attention and became a regular panelist and debater at Radio Uganda, which was by then the only radio station in Uganda. Invitations to speak in other districts all over the country quickly followed. The name 'Matembe' slowly but steadily gained countrywide recognition. I was not earning a salary, and sometimes I actually used my own meagre resources, but the sense of gratification and purpose that I derived from this work always urged me on.

Having grown into a national figure, it was not a surprise when people from Mbarara District encouraged me to represent them as a Woman Member of the National Resistance Council (NRC). In 1989, I was elected to represent Mbarara District in the NRC, which was the equivalent of Uganda's Parliament then.

This divine moment filled me with great joy. I felt that I had attained my long cherished dream; on top of being a lawyer, I was now a parliamentarian. I was now standing on the platform I had always desired, so that I could mobilise women and make laws that benefited them. At long last, my work could now begin.

# Chapter Two

## The Vicious Cycle of Human Stupidity and Early Cracks in the Movement

### Uganda's Chaotic Past

To appreciate the grave social, economic and political challenges in Uganda today, it is important that Uganda's turbulent history of brutality and authoritarianism is put into perspective. It is a widely known fact that in Uganda, there has never been a peaceful handover of power from one head of state to another. It is terribly sad that more than fifty years after independence, Ugandans are still yearning to experience the joy of witnessing a peaceful transition of government. Ours has always been a bloody affair.

Let me briefly list the men who have been at the helm of power in Uganda since Independence. After gaining self-rule on 9th October 1962, Uganda's first president was the Kabaka of Buganda, Sir Edward Mutesa II, with Dr Milton Obote as Prime Minister in an unholy marriage of convenience of the Kabaka Yekka party and UPC. It did not take long for squabbles and quarrels between the two to begin, culminating in the 1966 attack on the Lubiri, the Buganda king's palace, after the Kabaka said Obote should leave Buganda's soil. The Kabaka was forced to flee into exile in Britain like a commoner in circumstances that were far unbecoming of a king, let alone a president. Thereafter, Obote abrogated the constitution and proclaimed himself president.

In Uganda, whenever one leader has been deposed, a familiar scenario happens: kin and tribesmen of the deposed leader accused of 'eating the national cake' are persecuted, murdered or have to flee into exile. This pattern started after the attack on the Lubiri Palace by government troops. There was an immediate overthrow of government and therefore no handover of the instruments of power. Top Baganda royalists were not spared either; many followed their king into exile while others had to keep a low profile.

Similarly, in 1971 after Idi Amin deposed Obote in a coup d'etat, Amin's henchmen descended onto Obote's tribal allies – the Langi and Acholi. Many were murdered in cold blood while many others inevitably had to flee into exile. Around that time, I personally witnessed my parents hiding a Langi man under a millet cooking pot.

He was in our area under a government program for the eradication of tsetse flies. Luckily, under the cover of darkness, he found a way to escape to safety.

However, this was not before many Ugandans, especially the Baganda, lined the streets to jubilate upon the fall of Obote, whom they had never forgiven for desecrating their king and kingdom. They hailed Amin as their hero, despite the fact that the attack on the Lubiri had actually been led by Amin, at that time a senior military commander in Obote's administration.

In 1979, after the Uganda National Liberation Army (UNLA), supported by the Tanzanian army, overthrew Idi Amin, the pattern repeated itself. This time, Kakwa and Nubian army officers from West Nile who had been part of Amin's inner circle took to their heels and fled into exile.

Unfortunately, many ordinary people who were reportedly persecuted and punished at this time were not personally guilty of any wrongdoing; their only 'crime' was belonging to the same tribe as the deposed leaders.

When Obote returned to power following the highly disputed 1980 elections, we expected that at a minimum, in the aftermath of Amin's reign of terror, Obote would work to steady the country politically and economically. Unfortunately, having declared that he would "begin from where he left", Obote's government unleashed a new wave of malicious revenge and retribution against his perceived 'political enemies', as well as some of Amin's tribesmen who had not fled the country.

In Okello Lutwa's short-lived rule of Uganda,

similar vengeance was visited upon Obote's Langi soldiers, ordinary people and kinsmen by Lutwa's Acholi tribesmen. This vicious cycle of retribution against the 'eating tribe' (the tribe in power) is a sad chapter in our history that can only be reversed through free and fair elections and a peaceful transition of power from one president to another.

The optimism and general goodwill that ushered in President Museveni led many people, including myself, to believe that he would set a precedent for future leaders by preparing the country for an orderly and peaceful transfer of power. Alas! We have been massively let down.

## Early Signs of Dictatorship: *'Mzee Anapanga'*

Those who have known President Yoweri Museveni for a long time will tell you that his dictatorial tendencies did not spring upon us overnight. Many comrades *(as the early members of the NRA fondly refer to themselves),* have narrated different stories of how the dictatorial tendencies of Museveni sprouted very early during the struggle. My uncle, Hon Major John Kazoora, has shared with me some of these incidences of dictatorship during the Luweero war.

In the bush, there was a popular saying that, *'Mzee anapanga'* – a Kiswahili phrase that meant that it was only Museveni who planned. Therefore, his decision on anything was not open to any debate or scrutiny at all. This was so despite the fact that there were highly educated people within the rank and file of the NRA and that many young people had left university to join it. Whatever Museveni decided was to be taken as the gospel truth – to be obeyed and followed without any question, and yet every decision could have had far-reaching impact on the safety of them all because war is war and every member's life was in danger.

Unfortunately, even after the NRA/M captured power, Museveni continued to act and still acts like he did during the bush days. He is an almighty micro-manager who assumes the role of one who can solve everything. For example, why would a president spend millions of shillings on an upcountry trip simply because he wants to commission a borehole, as he has done many times? What then becomes of the role of the RDCs, LC5 chairpersons, CAOs and other civil servants in the local governments? I believe that he has totally failed to recover from 'the bush hangover' and still believes himself to be the all-knowing, all-powerful, all-conquering 'Ssabalwanyi' (The almighty fighter) and 'Ssabagabe' (King of Kings).

Even before he went to the bush, Museveni ensured he was in strategically powerful positions; for example, when Yusuf Lule died, Museveni became the Chairman of the National Resistance Council (NRC) which was in essence the Parliament. Further, he has been the Chairman of the Army High Command throughout his presidency. Even after the 1995 Constitution was promulgated, Museveni still suffered from that 'bush hangover',and he still acts like he wants to be the Speaker of Parliament even as he is the Head of the Executive. This is why he often interferes with the Legislature by holding ruling party caucuses at his State House to decide what Parliament must do.

In 1998, when Hon James Wapakabhulo became too independent-minded, Museveni removed him from the position of Speaker of Parliament. How does a President remove someone who has been elected by Parliament? That is when he brought in Hon Francis Ayume whom he thought he would control like a puppet.

This singular act of removing a bona fide Speaker of Parliament, I felt, did not get the condemnation that it deserved from the public. It was the highest imaginable abuse of Parliament and democratic principles because it totally disregarded the Constitution in terms of how a Speaker of Parliament can be legally removed. It was as bad, if not worse than the infamous *'rape of the temple of justice'* when the Black Mamba, a special paramilitary unit, stormed the High Court on 1st March, 2007 during the hearing of the Besigye bail application case to re-arrest five men who had been granted bail after fifteen months in detention. The men were part of a group of individuals known as the 'PRA suspects' who were charged with treason along with Dr Kizza Besigye for their alleged involvement in a rebel movement. Yet, at that time, people did not realize the full implication of how heinous that single act was in damaging the key tenets of democracy and the tripartite independent powers of the Executive, Legislature and the Judiciary.

Justice James Ogoola, an eyewitness of the raid and a Principal Judge at the time, described the incident as a "despicable act" and a "rape of the temple of justice". He added that, "The siege constituted a very grave and heinous violation of the twin principles of the Rule of Law and Judicial Independence. It sent a chilling feeling down the spine of the Judiciary, and left the legal fraternity and the general public agape with disbelief and wonderment."

## Early Signs of the Politics of Patronage and Corruption

I remember one early incident that exposed how President Museveni dealt with corruption. In his first Cabinet, there was a Minister for Veterinary Services called Hon Shem Masaba, who at one point said that the way his fellow ministers were behaving showed that they had other means of making money – in other words, that they were corrupt. Masaba came out and said this in public, naively believing he was making positive criticism in the spirit of the Movement. In the subsequent cabinet reshuffle, however, Masaba was dropped.

At around that same time, in 1992, President Museveni in a speech said: "I am convinced of the correctness of our handling of our economy, security and political matters in our country; the worry however is in connection with the corruption of our public officers. How can we hope to convince anyone of the rightness of our goals if our own people are violating our own goals? Corruption is a cancer which if not checked will hinder progress of all sectors of society."

How does one reconcile President Museveni's speech and his response to Hon Masaba's statement about corruption? This was a case of paying lip service to the cause with neither the will nor willingness to fight corruption or political games. Since then, the lip service has continued and, even, escalated. There have been occasions where a Public Accounts Committee (PAC) of Parliament investigates and finds someone in President Museveni's inner circle corrupt, but, in his characteristic style, the President has called the PAC members and asked them to shelve the report because it would damage NRM to expose and condemn such a person. That has been the way the cancer of corruption and patronage has gnawed at Uganda's tender flesh for far too long.

## 'Knowing Politics'

I got to learn over time that deep down in his heart, President Museveni does not really respect institutions nor does he respect the people he appoints or who are elected to head them. For him, it's a political game where every pawn serves a purpose for his own selfish ulterior motives. To him, being a president is the only difficult job. He believes that all other jobs, whether ministerial or below, can be done by anyone. It is only the presidency that requires special talent and skills. He has mastered the British colonial tactic of divide and rule, and he dishes out calculated appointments to appeal to and placate the different tribal, religious and even gender groups.

As members of the Ankole Parliamentary caucus in the early 2000s, we used to have meetings now and then to discuss varying topical issues in the country. On one specific occasion we were shocked by some of Museveni's revelations. Our caucus, chaired by Hon Eriya Kategaya and deputized by Hon Kahinda Otafiire, was believed to be very powerful. It seems President Museveni was trying to buy into that when he invited us to his Rwakitura home for a talk on how the Ankole region had influenced and shaped the politics of Uganda.

However, Museveni made statements like the following (and I paraphrase): This Kazibwe, you think she is a Vice President? How? What can she do? By appointing her, I kill many birds with one stone; the Basoga love me and think I am good because I have appointed one of their own as Vice President; the Catholics support me because I have appointed a Catholic as Vice President; the women, like Matembe here, are appeased and think I have done wonders because I have appointed one of their own. But surely, what can Dr Specioza Kazibwe do?

People were shocked but still laughed. And indeed, in practical terms, can anyone remember any significant role played by Dr Kazibwe in her capacity as a Vice President?

President Museveni went on: Look at Jeje Odongo, does he think he is an army commander? What army does he command? He cannot even transfer a section commander - the lowest commander. But when he goes to Teso with mounted jeeps, the people of Teso think their son has power, but where is it?

He went on to talk about David Pulkol, who was the Director of the External Security Organization (ESO) at that time. Look at this Karamajong; does he also think he gathers intelligence? When he goes in a helicopter and it lands and the Karamajong clamor to look at it, they are happy because their son is powerful. When I call him here, he tells me: "On one hand, Mr. President... and on the other hand..." and I fail to get which hand I should take! Just hopeless! But the Karamajong are very happy.

Hon John Kazoora shot up and asked, "Mr President, do you mean to say you don't have a Vice President, no Director of ESO, no Army Commander? Where is the government?"

President Museveni laughed, with that sarcastic laughter of his, and told Hon Kazoora that he had gathered us all there so that he would teach us how to manage politics. He went on to ridicule other ministers. He didn't have kind words for Hon Ruhakana Rugunda either. "Look at this Rugunda. Just posturing: '*Ndugu, Ndugu. Turabahereza amashanyarazi.*' (Meaning, we shall give you electricity). Do people eat electricity?"

I stood up and asked the President why he appointed old people and yet he kept complaining about their poor performance. I told the meeting that we got embarrassed while on foreign trips and these elderly ministers fell asleep in meetings and we got over-loaded trying to do our own work as well as represent them when they were, in fact, present. I mentioned the elderly people who should be retired, singling out people like Hon Mayanja Nkangi and Hon Kajura who had been ministers since my primary school days.

The President looked at me and laughed, saying, "You, Matembe, you are just a novice in politics. When I appoint Kajura, apart from securing Bunyoro region, the whole of Rubaga (the Catholic Church) is with me; when I appoint Nkangi, Buganda and the entire Namirembe (the Protestants) rally behind me. Leave my old men alone, let them sleep, but for me, they serve a critical purpose."

President Museveni added that Moses Ali took care of West Nile and the Moslem vote.

In essence, Museveni was saying that service delivery was never a key motivation for him. He was only interested in self-preservation and sustenance in power. Is it any wonder that these ministers just sleep away during key state functions like the State of the Nation Address, the Budget reading and so on, since they are not expected to perform? Lately, they have devised a method of chewing gum and wearing dark glasses. The whole spectacle has become comical, if not an irritant.

The point is that Museveni does not respect institutions. From the days of 'Mzee anapanga' to date, he has worked tirelessly to undermine every single institution and disenfranchise its leaders so as to perpetuate the politics of patronage. It is in his interest that he totally kills off the institutions so that, like the pre-French revolution King Louis XVI, he becomes the state, and the state becomes himself.

It is no surprise, therefore, that President Museveni declared publicly and in person that he has no friends. One time in 1997 while in a meeting with him at State House, Entebbe, he told me a story: that Prof George Kanyeihamba had at one time advised him to get a few close friends to form an inner circle that would advise him on issues of governing the country. President Museveni told me that he laughed it off and categorically told the professor that, for him, he had no friends. I sat there bewildered, because there I was, thinking that I was his friend!

# Chapter Three

# The Rattling of the Snake's Cage

## The Aftermath of Dr Besigye's Dossier – 'An Insider's View on How NRM Lost its Broad-Base'

When Dr Kizza Besigye declared his candidature for the presidency via a press release on Saturday, 28th October in 2000, it was a huge surprise, especially for us in the Movement. His move came a week after his 20th October, 2000 retirement from the army and a year after his November 1999 dossier entitled *"An Insider's View on How NRM Lost its Broad-Base."* The dossier revealed the weaknesses which had been noticed within the Movement government.

Dr Besigye played a key role in the NRA guerrilla war where he served as Museveni's personal doctor. After the NRA captured power in 1986, he was appointed a minister and also served as National Political Commissar – a position which made him a key ideologue of the Movement and also saw him once again working closely with the President.

In the highly publicized document, Besigye accused Museveni's 'Movement' of being undemocratic, corrupt, opportunistic, dishonest and sectarian. He also accused it of reneging on its core principles of individual merit and being broad-based. Besigye further said that the Movement had been manipulated by people seeking to gain or retain political power, and that it was behaving like a political party contrary to what it professed to be. The dossier is reproduced below verbatim.

## An Insider's View on How the NRM Lost the 'Broad-Base'

*I have taken keen interest and participated in the political activities on the Ugandan scene since the late 1970s. This was during a period of intense jostling to topple and later succeed the Idi Amin regime. I am, therefore, fully aware of the euphoria, excitement and hope with which Ugandans received the Uganda National Liberation Front/Army (UNLF/A). Ugandans supported the UNLF's stated approach of "politics of consensus" through the common front. It was hoped that the new approach to politics would be maintained and Uganda rebuilt from the ruins left by the Amin regime. Unfortunately, instead of nurturing the structures, and regulations which bound the front together, we witnessed a primitive power struggle that resulted in ripping the front apart to the chagrin of the population.*

*Some of us young people were immediately thrown into serious confusion. We had not belonged to any political party before, and we did not approve of the record and character of the existing parties – UPC and DP. Spontaneously, many people started talking of belonging to a Third Force. This force represented those persons who wished to make a fresh start at political organisation, with unity and consensus politics as the centre pin. With a few months left to the 1980 elections, the Third Force crystallized into a new political organisation– the Uganda Patriotic Movement (UPM). The population, to a large extent, expressed their appreciation of the ideas and opportunity presented by the young organisation, but was pessimistic regarding its electoral success.*

*Pessimism was justified, because the new organisation simply had no time and resources to organize effectively nationally; and UPC was already positioning itself very loudly and arrogantly to rig the elections and seemed to have what was essential for them to do so successfully. After the sham 1980 elections, when Paulo Muwanga, a leader of UPC (and chairman of the Military Commission) took over all powers of the Electoral Commission and declared his own election results, there was widespread despondency and tension. While the "minority" DP Members of Parliament took up the opposition benches in Parliament, the rank and file of the party rapidly united behind the new forces of resistance to struggle against the dictatorial rule. The Popular Resistance Army (PRA and later, NRA) led by Yoweri Museveni which started with about 30 fighters, was overwhelmed by people seeking to join its ranks. The NRM was born as a political organisation in June 1981.*

*It was created by a protocol that effected the merger of Uganda Freedom Fighters UFF (led by the late Prof Y.K. Lule and Museveni's PRA). The armed wing of the organisation became the National Resistance Army (NRA). The NRM political programme was initially based on seven points which were later increased to become the well-known Ten-Point Programme. The basic consideration in drawing up the programme was that it should form the basis of a broad national political and social force. A national coalition was considered to be of critical importance in establishing peace, security, and optimally moving the country forward. The political programme was, therefore, referred to as a minimum programme around which different political forces in Uganda could unite for rehabilitation and recovery of the country.*

*To achieve unity, it was envisaged that the minimum programme would be implemented by a broad-based government. After the bush war, discussions were undertaken with the various political forces to establish a broad-based government that would reflect a national consensus. The NRM set up a committee led by Eriya Kategeya (then chairman of the NRM Political and Diplomatic Committee) for the purpose of engaging the various groups in these discussions. This exercise was, however, never taken to its logical conclusion. It would appear that once the leaders of the political parties were given "good" posts in the NRM government, their enthusiasm for the discussions waned, and the process eventually fizzled out. In spite of the lack of a proper modus operandi, the initial NRM government (executive branch) was impressively broad-based. Consensus politics conducted through elections based on individual merit and formation of broad-based government became the hallmark of the NRM.*

### Broad base undermined

*However, the popular concept of the broad-based government, which had also received support of most political groups, was progressively undermined. It ought to be remembered that due to the support and cooperation of other political groups, no legal restrictions were imposed on political parties until August 11, 1992 when the NRC made a resolution on political party activities in the interim period. In my opinion, there were three factors responsible for undermining and later destroying the NRM cardinal principle of broad-basedness, especially in appointment to the Executive: the NRM had set itself to serve for a period of four years as an interim government, then return power to the people. However, it was not very clear how this would happen at the end of the four years.*

*Some politicians in the NRM government who came from other political parties set out to use their advantaged positions to, on the one hand, undermine the NRM and on the other, strengthen themselves in preparation for the post-NRM political period. Consequently, they fell out with the NRM leadership, and a number of them were arrested and charged with treason. Historical NRM politicians who thought that they were not "appropriately" placed in government, blamed this on the large number of the "non-NRM" people in high up places, and set out to campaign against the situation. They created a distinction between government leaders as "NRM", and "broad-based". If you were referred to as "broad-based", it was another way of saying that you were undeserving of your post, or that you were possibly an enemy agent ("5th Columnist").*

*After some years of NRM rule, some in the leadership began to feel that there was sufficient grassroots support for the NRM, such that one could "off-load" the "broad-based" elements in government at no political cost. These factors were at the centre of an unprincipled power-struggle which was mostly covert and hence could not be resolved democratically. It continued to play itself out outside the formal Movement organs, with the results of weakening and eventually losing the concept of consensus politics and broad-basedness. By the time of the Constituent Assembly elections that were held in 1994, the NRM's all encompassing, and broad-based concept remained only in name. For instance, while the CA electoral law clearly stated that candidates would stand on "individual merit", the NRM Secretariat set up special commercial committees at districts whose task was to recommend "NRM candidates" for support. Not only did the logistical and administrative machinery of NRM move against the candidates supporting or suspected to be favouring early return to multiparty politics, it even moved against liberal candidates advocating for the initial NRM broad-based concept.*

*That is why many people were surprised and confused when some senior NRM leaders declared that "we have won!" after the CA results were announced. Who had won? It was clear that there were two systems; one described in the law, and another being practised. Moreover, the conduct of the CA, again exhibited the contradictions between the principles of NRM (and the law), and the practice. I was quite alarmed when I read a document titled 'Minutes Of A Meeting Between H.E The President with CA Group Held On 25.8.94 At Kisozi.' The copy had been availed to me by my colleague Lt Col Serwanga Lwanga (RIP) who attended the meeting. Present at the meeting were recorded as: H.E. the President (Chair), Eriya Kategaya, Bidandi Ssali, Steven Chebrot, Agard Didi, George Kanyeihamba, Miria Matembe, Mathias Ngobi, Mr Sebalu, Lt Noble Mayombo, Jotham Tumwesigye, Aziz Kasujja, Beatrice Lagada, Faith Mwonda and Margaret Zziwa. The introduction of the meeting reads in part as follows: The National Political Commissar introduced this committee as a Constituent Assembly Movement Group which wants to agree on a common position.*

*The arbitrary hand-picked group went ahead to take positions on major areas of the draft constitution, which we members of CA, (considered as "NRM supporters"), were supposed to support in the CA. It is interesting to note that among the 16 hand-picked members of the group, only six were directly elected to represent constituencies in the CA. The others were presidential nominees and representatives of special interest groups. One member was not even a CA delegate. We strongly resisted this approach, and after intense pushing and shoving, this group was replaced by the "Movement Caucus" under the chairmanship of the National Political Commissar, Kategaya.*

### Changing Movement

*The Movement caucus acted very much like an organ of a ruling party. All ministers (except Paul Ssemogerere who later resigned from government) were members. The hand-picked group, and the Movement caucus after it, both undermined the principles of the Movement and the law. The Constituent Assembly was negatively influenced by executive appointments. In the middle of the CA proceedings, a cabinet reshuffle saw Speciosa Kazibwe elevated to the vice presidency, Kintu Musoke to premier and several other delegates appointed to ministerial posts. Many others were appointed to be directors of parastatal companies. It is my opinion that after these actions, some CA delegates took positions believed to attract the favourable attention of the executive. Most CA delegates also intended to participate in the elections that would immediately follow the CA.*

### This had two negative effects:

*Being aware of the previous role of the NRM Secretariat in elections, some CA delegates would be compromised to act in such a way as to win the support of the Secretariat in the forthcoming elections. Some CA delegates saw themselves as the first beneficiaries of the government structure and arrangements that were being constitutionalised. So, they took positions which would favour them, and not the common good. As a result, the CA progressively became polarized, and its objectivity was diminished, especially when dealing with political systems. For example, at the commencement of the CA, every delegate made an opening statement highlighting major views on the draft constitution. Analysis of these statements shows that few delegates supported the immediate introduction of multiparty system while the majority supported the continuation of the "Movement system" for a transitional period of varying length.*

*The positions expressed were very much in line with the views gathered by the Constitutional Commission. The commission noted in its report (paragraph 0.46) that a consensus on the issue could not be attained. This was demonstrated by the statistical analysis of views gathered from RC 1 to RC V, plus individual and group memoranda. It will be seen that nationally, at RC 1, "Movement" supporters were 63.2% and this percentage decreased progressively as they went to higher RCs until RCV (District Councils) where Movement supporters were only 38.9% and multiparty supporters were 52.8%. Among the individual memoranda, 43.9% supported a multiparty system, while 42.1% supported Movement. Among the group memoranda, 45.1% supported multiparty, while 41.4% supported Movement. It is important to note that these views were gathered at a time when there was no impending election, and therefore, no campaigning.*

*Accordingly, the Constitutional Commission proposed the following, as the only limitation on political party activities (in Article 98 of Draft Constitution): "For the period when the Movement is in existence, political parties shall not endorse, sponsor, offer platform to or in anyway campaign for or against any candidate for public office." The CA under the influences outlined earlier ended up with restrictions contained in the highly contentious article 269 of the Constitution. The character of the Movement gradually changed, and the process of change was not determined democratically. Instead, it was continuously manipulated. Established Movement organs were continuously undetermined, and others completely ignored. For example, the National Executive Committee (NEC) of NRM was the organ supposed to be coordinating change in the NRM, yet NEC had not met for more than three years prior to the promulgation of the 1995 constitution – in spite of a requirement for it to meet at least once every three months. Instead, covert and arbitrarily constituted groups came in, like district election committees, special CA groups, Movement Political High Command, Movement caucus, Maj Kakooza Mutale's group, etc. The Movement created by the CA and completed by Parliament (through the Movement Act 1997) was different from the one of 1986-1995.*

*The Movement Act 1997 created a political organisation with structures outside the governmental structure. For the first time, the Movement was a political organisation distinct from government, the only remaining link being that it was funded by the government. Unfortunately, instead of describing the Movement as a political organisation, the CA chose to call it a political system – distinct from "Multiparty Political System", and other systems that may be thought of later. This was, in my opinion, a grave error. We even ignored advice given to us through a letter by President Yoweri Museveni (chairman NRM and Commander in Chief NRA) to the CA-NRM caucus delegates, dated June 21, 1995. In the letter, the chairman says, "the NRM is not a state but a political organisation that tries to welcome all Ugandans. It therefore cannot coerce all Ugandans to be loyal to it. Loyalty to NRM is voluntary." The reality of the Movement today is that it is a political organisation in much the same way as any political party is. Having no membership cards does not make it less so. In fact, in the letter referred to above, President Museveni further explains: "then some people may ask the question, If NRM could be ready to compete for political office with opposing political forces in future, why not do it now? Do not support doing it now because it is not in the best [interest] of governance and fortunately now the people still agree with us. It is only when the majority of the people change that we have to adjust our position. It would be something imposed on us by circumstances." So the NRM/Movement system is a convenient and, for the time, popular means to political power.*

## Manipulation

The characteristics which made the NRM government popular, such as the broad-based strategy, principle of individual merit, and the 10-Point Programme have been seriously eroded. This is evidenced by the bitter antagonism and animosity which exists between Movement supporters in many parts of the country, e.g. Kabale, Ntungamo, Kasese and Iganga. After more than 13 years of NRM rule, armed rebellion rages on in northern Uganda, and has also become entrenched in the western part of the country. All in all, when I reflect on the Movement philosophy and governance, I can conclude that the Movement has been manipulated by those seeking to gain or retain political power, in the same way that political parties in Uganda were manipulated. Evidently, the results of this manipulation are also the same, to wit: Factionalism, loss of faith in the system, corruption, insecurity and abuse of human rights, economic distortions and eventually decline. So, whether it's political parties or Movement, the real problem is dishonest, opportunistic and undemocratic leadership operating in a weak institutional framework and a weak civil society which cannot control them.

I have shown that over the years the "Movement System" has been defined in the law in a certain way, but the leaders have chosen to act in a different way. This is dishonest and opportunistic leadership. I have also shown how changes have been made to the Movement agenda, and other important decisions have been made outside the Movement structures. This too is undemocratic leadership.

*In my opinion, the way forward in developing a stable political situation is to do the following: Urgently revisit the legal framework with a view to making an equitable law and regulation for all political organisations. The Movement should be treated as a political organisation. Implementing this would need amendments to the Constitution, including amendment of articles 69 and 74. This requires the approval of the people through a referendum and the forthcoming referendum could be used for this purpose. In any case, laws are a reflection of the political will, so if there is political will to correct a situation, finding a way is easy.*

*The primary guarantor of democracy, human rights and the rule of law must be the civil society. Its capacity should, therefore, be quickly developed. Focus on a programme that could quickly raise the standards of living of our people to a decent level. This is an essential antecedent for our society to build a viable democracy. Of course, the approach to raising the standards of living is highly debatable. I have personal views that I hope to share with the public at another time. I pray to the almighty God to guide us so that we do not stumble again.*

### KIZZA BESIGYE

This document angered President Museveni so much and it caused a very big rift between him and Dr Besigye. President Museveni even threatened to arrest Dr Besigye. It took the intervention and pressure of elders from Rukungiri District, who went to State House to plead for Dr Besigye, to prevent the arrest. However, while the elders managed to avert the impending arrest, they were unable to reconcile the two.

What Besigye revealed in his dossier was not news to many of us in the Movement. As Members of Parliament from Ankole, our caucus had on several occasions discussed the weaknesses and problems that our government faced. In several meetings, we had brought such problems to the attention of the President who promised to set time to enable us discuss those matters in detail. But I believe he was simply buying time because he never really wanted to entertain any criticism that NRM was veering off its original path.

However, we in the Movement had never discussed these matters in terms of the succession to the presidency. So when Besigye declared his candidature, we were taken by surprise; of course, we were not ready for it. Whereas we had been discussing the same issues that Dr Besigye raised in his dossier, we had not envisaged that someone would emerge from within the Movement to challenge President Museveni in the elections. As a matter of fact, the Movement caucus chaired by Prof Gilbert Bukenya decided to invite Dr Besigye to discuss his dossier. We were gathered at the Conference Centre and expected Dr Besigye to address us, only to see President Museveni storm into the hall, in military fatigues saying how could Dr Besigye address the Movement caucus.

It is true that we had been bothered and concerned for some time about the President's growing dictatorial tendencies, the increasing levels of impatience and intolerance, the narrowing down of the political space, and the rising levels of corruption within the Movement government. Our main concern at that time was the need to clean up the Movement and get it back on the right track; the original track. This was the view of all the MPs from Ankole.

The reason why we were concerned was clear. The political history of Uganda has been such that whenever a President from any tribe has messed up the country and is removed, his sins are visited unto his whole tribe and region of origin, as alluded to in the previous chapters. So, we the Banyankore also wanted to save ourselves from the likely outcome of bad leadership. We thought it was incumbent upon us to prevent President Museveni from going astray because we knew that the consequences of his bad leadership would be visited upon people from his tribe and region once he was out of office. We wanted to deal with these problems before it would be too late.

We had also expressed a desire that it would be best if President Museveni did not contest for the presidency again in 2001. The truth is that we were not happy about the general state of democracy in the country. However, we were still hopeful that we could iron out things through dialogue with the President.

It was against this state of affairs that Dr Besigye declared his intention to stand for the presidency. It certainly caught us by surprise and I am sure it surprised the President too because it sent him crazy. Yes, I personally was surprised by Dr Besigye's announcement, but I was extremely shocked by President Museveni's reaction to

Dr Besigye's declaration of his intention.

The President was so furious, it was as if Besigye had committed the most heinous crime imaginable on earth. "How can he? How dare he? Who does he think he is to challenge me?" These were the kind of statements President Museveni made. I think this was the first time it ever occurred to him that anybody in the Movement could dare challenge his hold onto power.

President Museveni was so incensed, it was as if heaven itself had fallen down. The Banyankore would say *"ngu akagwe kaagwa"*– as if the abominable had happened. I think that is when I first saw this 'chief' in his true colours. He was like a wild cat under attack! He took the issue so personally that he viewed it as an act of extreme arrogance and impudence on the part of Besigye. How could he dare challenge him? This is when Museveni demonstrated his highest level of egoism. The *Ssabagabe* ran amok. He called a Cabinet meeting and put forward some really ludicrous proposals, urging us to enact a law that would bar Dr Besigye from contesting. We could not believe our ears when Museveni suggested that we should amend the law to make it mandatory for anybody seeking the Presidency to be tested for HIV/AIDS. It took a lot of convincing for us to sober him up. Thank God, by then he still had an ear to listen, at least, not like now, when he seems to listen to nobody. We assured him that we were with him and so he should cool down. We told him this was not the end of the world.

That is the first time I realized that Museveni's love for power had become an addiction. He was getting terribly paranoid. At that time, he resorted to writing missive after missive in the newspapers that really exposed him like a scared teenager. I remember that I, personally, advised him to stop writing his letters to the press. I reminded him of the Kinyankore proverb: *"ngu oine embwa tayemokyera"*, which means, if you own a dog, you do not do the barking for yourself.

I tried to convince him that since he had us, his ministers and supporters, he should maintain his dignity as the President and Fountain of Honour instead of indulging in rather petty quarrels with Dr Besigye. We told him to let his press secretary and other such officials deal with the press.

Amidst all this, Dr Besigye's daring decision helped unmask President Museveni as a megalomaniac. Moreover, he had no genuine reason to act that way; what crime had Besigye committed? I, personally, saw nothing wrong with Besigye's action. According to the National Constitution, Dr Besigye met all the qualifications required to contest for the presidency.

The problem was that President Museveni had never envisaged that any of his colleagues within the Movement would challenge him. He did not mind being challenged by any of the politicians from the other parties. He knew that parties such as UPC or DP did not have much credibility and support from the people, and such a contest would be a walk-over for him. However, a candidate from within the Movement could be a real challenge. This incident exposed Museveni as a leader who has a special phobia for elections. As events have turned out even now, President

Museveni does not and cannot allow any member of his party to contest against him for the presidency.

A similar pattern was later to emerge with President Museveni's fallout with former Prime Minister Hon Amama Mbabazi because he dared to contest against Museveni in 2015 within the NRM. The president went all the way to sponsor MPs like Hon Evelyn Anite to declare him the sole candidate. He left no stone unturned in his schemes of using his so-called young cadres to attack, abuse and humiliate Mbabazi who was a long-time confidante of his. This is the very President Museveni who swore to all and sundry at the wedding of Hon Kahinda Otafiire's son at Munyonyo that for the service they had rendered to him over the years, Kahinda Otafiire and Amama Mbabazi were untouchable. He said that he would never forsake them for their role in the founding of FRONASA and NRM.

As a matter of fact, Museveni vehemently defended Mbabazi as 'Mr. Clean' during the scandals of the Temangalo land sale and the oil companies licensing bribery where he was allegedly improperly involved. Museveni went a mile further to reward MPs like Perez Ahabwe and Hope Mwesigye, who stood by Mbabazi at that time, with ministerial appointments. From the Museveni-Amama relationship, therefore, it is easy to infer that the only unforgivable 'sin' against Museveni is challenging his hold on power.

One wonders then, if Museveni has done such marvelous wonders for Uganda, and is so loved, why would he want to deny himself the joy and satisfaction of winning an election; even, at least, the primaries of his own party? Now everybody within the Movement party knows they dare not challenge him, which is why he stands unopposed.

## Ankole Caucus Meets Dr Besigye

As the acrimony between President Museveni and Dr Besigye continued to grow, we, the Ankole caucus, decided to discuss the issues with Dr Besigye with the intention of reconciling him and President Museveni. The meeting was held at the Ministry of Public Service, where Hon Amanya Mushega was minister, and was chaired by Hon Eriya Kategaya. The caucus was constituted of seventeen MPs from the then Mbarara, Bushenyi and Ntungamo districts. We had an additional responsibility to attempt to diffuse this conflict between the two men from our region, especially since MPs from the other regions were asking us for the way forward.

We had a lengthy and candid meeting with Dr Besigye, where he told us why he had decided to challenge President Museveni in running for the presidency. The reasons were more or less the same as those we had already discussed within our caucus: the fact that the leadership of the Movement was veering away from its original vision and was becoming undemocratic and dictatorial. Dr Besigye's view was that since President Museveni seemed to be the main problem, and he was not ready to either change his style of leadership or to give up his seat, somebody had to contest against him and save the country from degenerating into a total dictatorship.

Dr Besigye told us he was not dying to be the president of Uganda, but, at the very least, he wanted somebody to come up and give Museveni a formidable challenge. He said he was ready to withdraw his bid and support anybody within the Movement who was ready to challenge Museveni. However, he was emphatic that as long as there was nobody else to do that, he was determined to continue with his bid.

We were in agreement with Dr Besigye on the fact that the Movement government was clearly getting off the democratic path and sidelining its original vision. However, we did not agree with him on the issue of contesting against President Museveni. We reasoned that although we concurred that things were not going well, and in fact we had been informing the President of this, we had not addressed ourselves to the issue of succession. So his bid for the presidency had caught us unawares. Besides, since he had not even consulted or informed us about it, we found it difficult to simply give him our support. If it was a question of who would take over the presidency from Museveni, it would only be proper for the leadership of the Movement to discuss and decide on the new flag bearer in an organised and democratic manner.

Our view was that according to the country's Constitution, President Museveni had only one more term to run, and since we had not yet discussed the issue of who would be our next candidate, it was only proper to let him run for this one more time. Granted, he was becoming dictatorial, less tolerant of divergent views, and more tolerant of corruption; still, we all agreed that he had done quite well in previous years. True, just like any other human being, he had made some mistakes.

We had actually thought that Museveni would probably not contest in the 2001 general elections, but since he expressed an interest to do so, we thought we could not just abandon him abruptly, just like that. We suggested to Dr Besigye that he should let President Museveni run unopposed for only the next one term. We hoped that within that last term, we could discuss issues and bring the Movement back on track, and also deal with the issue of succession. We tried to convince Dr Besigye to agree with us, but he did not find our reasons convincing. He said that if we ever thought that Museveni had any intentions of leaving power after his last term, we were day-dreaming.

Dr Besigye insisted that he was only prepared to abandon his bid if somebody else was willing to contest against President Museveni. He told us that anybody who thought Museveni could ever leave power willingly was joking. In hindsight, how accurate Dr Besigye was in his assessment of Museveni!

## President Museveni's Stance on the Constitution

I had such a high trust in Museveni that at no time had I thought that he could either think or dream of ever changing the national constitution to extend his stay in power.

The problem I have found with people like myself, who seem to have a genuine childlike and naive trust, is that the impact of the betrayal of our trust is shattering. The betrayal does not only make us withdraw our trust completely from those we had trusted; we also tend to withhold it from anybody else in their category. We learn to view everybody with suspicion, which is not good at all. Unfortunately that is what has happened to me. These days I am reminded of the biblical scripture in John 2:24, where it says that Jesus never entrusted His life with anybody because He knew the hearts of human beings.

If there was anybody who had been so deceived and betrayed by the President, it was me. First, I had been a member of the Uganda Constitutional Commission chaired by Justice Benjamin Odoki that had prepared the draft constitution. During this exercise which took us four years from 1989 to 1992, I had very close interactions with Museveni as we discussed constitutional issues. He used to invite me to his office to brief him on how the exercise was going. He gave me the impression that he was committed to constitutionalism because he had once told me that if there was anything that he would bequeath to Ugandans, it was a good constitution. So now that we had got the good thing that he had so desired to bequeath to Ugandans, which was promulgated on 8th October 1995, how could I have imagined that he could think of abusing and tampering with it?

Secondly, sometime in 2002, I had a brief telephone conversation with President Museveni on the issue of removing the constitutional term limits, in which he assured me that he was committed to constitutionalism. The telephone conversation was instigated by some remarks I had made at a regional women's conference on peace and security within the Great Lakes Region. The conference was held in Kampala at Hotel Equatoria. I was invited as the Guest of Honour to open the conference which had brought together women from the entire region.

The conference discussed the role of women in peace building, conflict prevention and resolution. During that period the region was overwhelmed with conflicts in Uganda, Burundi and the DRC. It also coincided with the time when President Chiluba of Zambia attempted to remove the presidential term limits from the National Constitution of Zambia. Chiluba's bid failed after he was vehemently opposed by members of parliament, in spite of the fact that many had been harassed, intimidated and others imprisoned.

In my opening address, I told the women that one of the causes of conflicts in Africa was the prolonged stay in power of our leaders who were ready to use any means, including violence against any opposition, to stay in power. They become greedy not only for power, but also for wealth; and, as a result, become dictators who resort to politics of patronage, intimidation, militarism and exclusion. I added that such leaders lose the ability to fight corruption and any other form of injustice because their addiction to power makes them vulnerable and hostage to the corrupt who help to sustain them in power.

I told them that countries that have undergone democratisation processes have taken advantage of these processes to constitutionally limit presidential terms so as to prevent the notion of life presidency. I went on to say that even with this safety net, the African leaders do not seem to learn, as evidenced by Zambia's Chiluba who was fighting to remove term limits so that he could stay in power. I appealed to the women to make sure that they fight such a tendency in their countries as a way of preventing conflict. I told the women that in Uganda we were lucky to have a good president who was committed to constitutionalism. He knew the value of a good constitution to a nation and that was why he had championed its making. He also believed in the term limits.

I went on to say that however, we can never be sure with human beings. We can never know what a leader can do once power enters his head, since it is said that power corrupts. "Should he ever want to remove our presidential constitutional term limits, I call upon you, women of Uganda, to oppose him because removing the presidential term limits would be a recipe for chaos and conflict in this country again. If you women do not rise to oppose him, I will do it myself, even if I have to do it alone," I declared to the conference attendees.

As I said all this, little did I know that I was giving news to the press. The very next day, a cartoon appeared in one of the Ugandan dailies showing President Museveni seated in his office, and there I was, holding a bell in his face. The cartoon's caption was: "2006, Mr. President, time's up."

At about midday on the same day, when I was in a Cabinet meeting, the Principal Private Secretary to the President, Ms Hilda Musubire, called me out saying that the president wanted to speak to me. I went to her office, picked the phone and said, "Your Excellency sir, this is Matembe on the line."

As usual, he started, *"Matembe, oreire ota? Emirimo wagihitsyahi?"*- Meaning, "Matembe, how are you, and how is work?"

*"Ndyaho Ssebbo, nemirimo negyendagye,"* I said, meaning, "I am alright and work is going on well." In fact, most of the time when he called me, we spoke in Runyankore.

He went on: *"Beitushi, kandi kanakureeba nondagiira,"* meaning that he had seen me ordering him around.

"Sir, how can I order you around? These days I do not talk much, I am a bit quiet. I am busy doing my job. So your people are once again telling you lies about me? When did I order you? In any case, order you to do what? *Ebyo Matembe ndareebire* (I, Matembe, have really suffered)."

When he heard me getting anxious, he said, "No, no Matembe, relax, do not worry; I am just seeing this picture where you are ordering me."

"Which picture, sir?" I asked.

"The picture in the newspaper," he replied. I told him I had not yet looked at the day's newspapers therefore I didn't know the picture he was talking about. I asked him whether it was a cartoon.

"Yes, there is a cartoon here where you are ringing a bell for me and telling me to quit the office of the president because my time is up," he replied.

I asked Ms Musubire to give me the paper and I checked it, only to find that it was about the statement I had made at the women's conference the previous day.

"Sir, you know these press people know how to twist things. They are trying to portray what I was saying at the Great Lakes Region women's conference on peace and security yesterday."

He said, "Okay, tell me what you said."

I told him what I said at the conference, about my intention to oppose him if he ever attempted to amend the constitution to remove term limits, like Chiluba was trying to do in Zambia.

"Why are you imputing bad motives onto me? You think I do not know when to leave office? Should it be you to tell me?"

"Sir, I am sorry. I really had no intention of imputing ill motives onto you. I was only saying that should you feel like you have not completed your program and you want to stay on a little longer, I would remind you of your commitment to the constitution. But that was just a statement; I know you know when to leave," I replied.

"You see, Matembe, I also know this constitution, and after all, I am the one who appointed you to the Constitutional Commission. Therefore, I am also aware that there is a constitution and I have no intention of violating it," he assured me.

Museveni had at around that time just returned from England where he had been interviewed by the BBC as to whether he would seek re-election in 2006, and he had maintained that he would stick to the constitution. President Museveni is so cunning in that whenever he was asked whether he would leave power in 2006, he always answered that he would stick to the constitution because he knew he was going to change it. He never answered this question in the negative or affirmative.

So during the telephone conversation I told him, "Your Excellency, I know you know the constitution and you intend to stick to it, as you recently said in your interview with the BBC. If what I said innocently at the conference annoyed you please forgive me, I did not intend to hurt your feelings."

"You see Matembe, when you talk like that, you create an impression that I do not know what I ought to know and it is other people to tell me. I do not have to be pressurized out of office because I too know the law. So there is a need to correct the impression that you have created. Write a letter to the New Vision editor so as to remove the wrong impression that your statement has created about me."

Immediately after the cabinet meeting, I wrote the letter to the Editor, New Vision. It was published the next day with a heading: 'Cartoon Creates a Wrong Impression'. In the letter I wrote that: "The cartoon created a wrong impression about the president, imputing that the president wants to amend the constitution to remove the presidential term limits. President Museveni knows the constitution very well and he does not need anybody to remind him to stick to it. So he will honour the constitution and will not in any way violate or abrogate it." I am sure he read that letter and was happy.

On that day, after my conversation with him, something shocked me about the personality of President Museveni. After the cabinet meeting, we learnt that Museveni's mother had passed away. Can you imagine that by the time we spoke, he already knew about his mother's death, and yet there he was, bothered about a cartoon? And he never told me about his loss at all! One would expect any normal person to take some time to grieve and at least inform his close colleagues about the death of his mother.

So after all this talk with Museveni, which gave me even more assurance and confidence that he meant to stick to the constitution, how could I not believe that he was going to quit come 2006?

## We Are Not Seeking Another Term, the First Lady Assures Me

Way back in 1996, the First Lady, Janet Museveni herself had told me that her husband was not going to run for the presidency again, even in 2001. After the presidential and district women representatives elections, but before the parliamentary ones (at that time there were different voting days for each category of election), the First Lady called me to their home in Rwakitura. We sat alone in a beautiful little hut and had a nice chat.

As born-again Christians, we prayed and thanked God for having been so kind and merciful to her family– for enabling her husband to come out of 'the bush' alive; for having given him the opportunity to resurrect this country from the ravage it had been in; for enabling us to make a good national constitution under which we had been able to conduct free and fair national elections, something that had not happened for 34 years by then. We praised God for having granted us success in the elections.

The President and I had already won in our respective elections. The First Lady and I were praying and anxiously waiting for Hon Elly Karuhanga, who had contested for the Nyabushozi MP seat, to also win. He and I were the First Lady's close confidants in Mbarara District.

It was at this time that Janet Museveni told me that since God had been so gracious to them and had now rewarded their efforts with the people's love and support, by which they had elected the President with an overwhelming majority vote of 75%, they were now satisfied with serving only one term and would retire in 2001.

I said, "Eh, you mean the President will not contest elections again even when the constitution allows him one more term?"

She replied, *"Mbwenu hati ekindi nituba nitwendaki?"* Meaning, what else would we want? She added that they had liberated the country and had started rebuilding it. They would use the next five years to consolidate the gains they had made for this country and then let somebody else hold the mantle. "We also need rest,"she said, "to be together with our family and enjoy the rest of our lives at this farm relaxing, with no worries about running the country."

"Are you sure of that?" I asked her. She replied that it was true; they had already discussed it as a family.

Of course I believed her, especially because she is a born-again Christian. I told her that for that matter, I might also not run again since I shall have done enough, having started serving in 1986 upon the assumption of power by the National Resistance Movement.

Having had such personal discussions with these two distinguished individuals holding such offices of honour, I would have to be a doubting Thomas not to believe them; I was certainly not a Thomas. In any case, I, as a born again Christian, was guided in my trust in them by the principle expounded by Jesus Himself when He said that: 'Blessed are those who believe without seeing' (John 20:29). And so I believed what they told me.

## The Life Presidency Project

**"** The man has no plans of going," Dr Besigye had fore-warned us. Armed with all this unfortunate false assurance, I had told Dr Besigye that he was imputing ill motives on the President to think that he would cling onto power beyond the constitutional term limits.

Little did I know that what Besigye had said was right. No wonder he said it; he had been in the bush with this man and had been his personal doctor. He had been close to him, had worked under him holding different portfolios, but somewhere along the line they had fallen out with each other. As for me, who had not known Museveni for that long and had not yet fallen out with him, I still had trust and confidence in him and so was not ready to abandon him. Together with the Ankole caucus and other colleagues, I was ready to give him another chance.

After failing to convince Besigye to give Museveni the benefit of doubt, we parted company with him and he continued on with his bid for the presidency while we went on to campaign for Museveni in his 2001 election bid.

At the start of Besigye's bid for the presidency, many people trivialized it saying Besigye was fighting Museveni because of a personal conflict between them. But some of us knew that Besigye had genuine reasons for his bid, even though we thought it was not the right time for it.

In fact, one problem that has been critical in constraining people's understanding of the real issues of bad governance in Museveni's government is the spin of personalizing disagreements between Museveni and his opponents, and yet they have disagreed on matters of principle. For example, when Besigye openly criticized Museveni's government for veering off the democratic path, people claimed that the real issue was a personal problem between him and Museveni, in particular over Hon Winnie Byanyima, who is said to have once been

Museveni's girlfriend, but later became Besigye's wife.

Similarly, when I, together with my colleagues Eriya Kategaya, John Kazoora, Richard Kaijuka, Amanya Mushega and Augustine Ruzindana disagreed with Museveni over the issue of presidential term limits, some people from other regions such as Busoga, Northern Uganda and Buganda trivialized our disagreement, which was based on principle, as merely being a personal matter between Museveni and his Banyankore colleagues. Some MPs from Busoga and Buganda went as far as to ask us why we were fighting 'our man' as if they could not see the wrong things that were going on in the country!

In any case, what personal issues were there that would cause a conflict between us and Museveni? There was and there continues to be nothing personal between us and Museveni. We are simply not happy with the way he has hijacked the country to suit his personal whims. We were duty bound to call out our brother to reason so as to save ourselves from any negative consequences of his undemocratic and unjust rule that would possibly fall on those from his tribe or region in the future. But there was, and continues to be, absolutely nothing personal about our disagreement with him over the removal of the presidential term limits.

Whenever anybody highly placed within the NRM government noticed a wrong and pointed it out, others said she or he was disgruntled. To date, this kind of cheap politics has persisted. Of course, it is believed to be propagated by Museveni himself and amplified through government loudspeakers such as Frank Tumwebaze,

Tamale Mirundi, Ofwono Opondo and others. It is diversionary. It is silly. It is deceitful. It is killing our country.

Anyway, Besigye went ahead and contested against Museveni in the 2001 general elections. Most of us, leaders from Ankole, did not support Besigye. This was because, although we were aware of Museveni's pitfalls, we had not organised ourselves for a change in leadership. We had decided, instead, to give him the benefit of the doubt; trusting and believing that he was running for his last term. Having done so well in lifting our country out of the ditch it was in when he took over the government in 1986, we felt that he was entitled to an honorable exit. Like any other person, he was bound to err, but as long as he was about to leave the presidency, it was okay with us. Besides, we had hopes that after winning elections in 2001, he would be willing to reorganize the Movement and put it back on its democratic path, while preparing for an orderly succession of leadership, as the country opened up to multiparty politics. In all this, we were fortified by the fact that President Museveni, in his 2001 Presidential Election Manifesto had openly and categorically on Page nine put it on record that it would be his second and last term in office.

Alas, two years later, in 2003, at the NRM National Executive Committee (NEC) conference at Kyankwanzi, President Museveni proposed the removal of the presidential term limits of ten years from the Uganda Constitution. Dr Besigye was proved right! I was very shocked and extremely sad and was so angry that I had been made such a fool of, to have placed my confidence in this man who clearly did not deserve it. I felt so betrayed after his proposal, especially when I talked to one individual after another who agreed with his bid to amend the constitution so as to give him an open bid for a life presidency.

I could not believe that this was the same man who had castigated African leaders who clung onto power. During those two days of debate on this issue, I listened to individuals glorifying and idolizing the man as he amusedly nodded to their appellations and praises. I simply could not believe that this was the man I had followed since 1986. At that moment, as I looked at President Museveni and compared him to other past leaders that he had been quick to brand as "swine", it was just like that incident in George Orwell's *Animal Farm*, when at a party the other animals looked at a man and looked at a pig and they saw no difference. It was sad.

I concluded then that this was the way dictators were made. I, however, made up my mind that even if I was the only one who was going to oppose Museveni's proposal, I would definitely do so.

# Chapter Four

## Insider Cliques, Manipulation and 'Us' Against 'Them'

### Sponsoring a Candidate against Me

The presidential campaigns of 2001 were a rude awakening for me as I first came face to face with the deceit, dishonesty and wickedness of the treacherous system I was serving. After campaigning for President Museveni against Dr Besigye, I was so shocked to learn that the very people I was with while campaigning for Museveni had got a candidate to stand against me and were campaigning for her in the parliamentary elections.

In fact, they were not fighting me alone; they also fought Hon. Major Kazoora of Kashaari and Bernadette Bigirwa of the then Bushenyi District. I came to understand later that this was part of the grand plan to remove the presidential term limits after the elections. The President and his clique were well aware that we were not in favour of lifting the presidential term limit and so it would be easier for them if we failed to get into parliament.

The President and his people therefore planted and sponsored candidates against us. They got candidates who they knew would never oppose the removal of the term limit because they would have to pay allegiance to those political godfathers who got them into parliament in the first place. Can you imagine the treachery? After working so hard in the presidential election campaigns, the very people I was fighting for stabbed me in the back!

Another reason I was being fought was because of my commitment to fighting corruption. When I was appointed the pioneer Minister for Ethics and Integrity in 1998, I was responsible for fighting corruption and building ethics and integrity in public offices. There were several high profile corruption scandals that my ministry had to deal with. Some of these cases involved people closely associated with the President.

There was the Uganda Commercial Bank case involving his brother, Salim Saleh. There was the Uganda Railways case involving some of his friends such as Enos Tumusiime. And there were other two cases involving senior ministers who were very close to the President and his family who were censured soon after I had assumed office. These were Hon Sam Kutesa, at the time Finance State Minister, who was censured in March 1999 for alleged misuse of office and influence peddling - 247 of the 276 MPs participated in the vote with 154 MPs voting for his censure while 94 supported him and; Hon Jim Muhwezi, State Minister in charge of Primary Education who was censured for alleged abuse of office after Parliament raised a red flag over his wealth - 148 MPs voted in favour of censuring Muhwezi while 91 supported him.

Some of these people were seeking re-election to parliament. In one of Museveni's worst mockery of Uganda's anti-corruption efforts, ironically, the two were later to bounce back to cabinet as full Cabinet Ministers. Sam Kutesa as Minister for Foreign Affairs and Jim Muhwezi as Minister for Health, where again he was involved in the Global Fund scandal that rocked the nation. **Note:** *Much later, Hon Sam Kutesa was in 2019 implicated in a very embarrassing corruption and bribery saga involving Patrick Ho, a Chinese national accused and convicted by the US Federal courts of bribing some African heads of state and Kutesa when he served as the President of the UN General Assembly.*

During that time, Uganda was highly profiled internationally as a country that was taking big steps to fight corruption because in addition to censured ministers, we had prosecuted a former Minister for Justice, as well as prosecuted and imprisoned a member of parliament, a permanent secretary and an undersecretary - all for corruption. So we were being viewed as serious because we were 'catching the big fish'.

When I returned from the second Global Forum on fighting corruption that was held in the Netherlands in 2001, and where Uganda was highly applauded for those bold steps in fighting corruption, I addressed a press conference in Kampala. At the conference, I was asked whether it was proper for censured ministers and other people implicated in corruption scandals to contest in the elections. I told the press that it would be good if the censured ministers and those implicated in corruption cases were not elected. Although some of these people were accused of corruption and unethical conduct, they were not convicted because prosecution and conviction demands watertight evidence, which is not easily available in many of the corruption cases. However, the country had lost so much as a result of the conduct of these fellows, that it would make a mockery of the citizens if such people were elected to parliament.

I appealed to the electorate to reject them during elections. Since they had not been convicted, the law did not bar them from contesting, but the electorate could reject them as unfit to represent them. I called upon the public to exercise their oversight role and reject anybody implicated or associated with corruption. I was very enthusiastic about keeping Uganda's flag flying high; little did I know that I was offending the powers that be, including the President. Following my call, the *Daily Monitor* newspaper published an article with the headline, *"Do Not Elect Censured Ministers" says Matembe*. The article came out on the very day that parliamentary campaigns kicked off and some of the names of those that were not to be elected appeared in the article.

I could understand why these big shots were angry with me since my work was interfering with their interests. But what shocked me was that my commitment and enthusiasm to fight corruption could anger the President! Why was I shocked? Because when the President appointed me as the Minister for Ethics and Integrity, I believed that he was committed to fighting corruption. Why? Because if you are not committed, you don't give the job to a big mouth like Matembe who is not prepared to cover up for anybody. So when the President appointed me, knowing that I am very outspoken, I thought, yeah, this guy is really committed to fighting corruption, otherwise he would not have risked putting me there.

## President Museveni's Abetting of Corruption: A Tale of the 'Untouchables'

I realized that I was dealing with the wrong guy when President Museveni got angry with me for calling upon the electorate to reject the censured ministers. First, I got a telephone call from Hon Sam Kutesa in the middle of the night. I was in Mbarara at that time, where I had gone to start my campaigns for the 2001 parliamentary elections . We had a long discussion, and he showed how angry he was with me by saying things like: "You are killing me; how can you kill my political life by saying that I should not be elected?"

He requested me to write to the press and withdraw my statement. I told him, "Look, I was giving a statement as head of my ministry, where I am supposed to be fighting corruption. When people ask me whether censured ministers should be elected, you don't expect me to say, go and elect them, do you? I am not withdrawing the statement."

He was infuriated and he warned me that, "If you are not careful, and if you do not withdraw the statement, I will finish you."

I asked him how he would finish me? Did he intend to kill me? He said: "I will kill you."

I told him that if he killed me, he will have saved me from these worldly troubles that I was going through. He replied, "I will not kill you physically, but I will destroy you politically."

"How will you kill me politically when you will not find any offence to accuse me of that can destroy me politically?" I asked him. I told him that the worst he could do to me was to falsely accuse me of sleeping around with men. I told him that if he did that, people would not believe him and would shun him as a result, and so my reputation would continue to flourish and he would not have managed to kill me.

By this time, some people within the Movement, especially from the President's family had already sponsored a candidate, one Ms Jovia Rwakishumba, to run against me. They, including Ms Kellen Kayonga and her sister Mrs Jovia Saleh, the President's sister-in-law, were carrying her around in my constituency on campaigns with a lot of money because they did not want me to win, despite the fact that I had supported and campaigned for Museveni.

So, in that same phone call, I told Kutesa that after all if it was about killing me politically, he had already done so since he had sponsored a candidate against me. He asked, "Who has sponsored a candidate against you?" I told him, "the State House you are a party to." He asked me how I knew. I told him that the chief agent was Mrs Jovia Saleh (the wife of Museveni's brother, Salim Saleh). I added that when Rwakishumba came for the nomination, she was accompanied by State House operatives and one of the President's confidants in Mbarara. Kutesa told me that he was not aware of that, and he too was concerned about his position and he urged me again to withdraw my public statement. We ended in disagreement because I stuck to my guns and told him that I was not going to withdraw the statement.

This issue of people who were my "allies" sponsoring a candidate against me had hurt me so much. By the time of Kutesa's phone call, I had discussed the issue with General Salim Saleh, his wife and her sister Kellen Kayonga, who were the ones taking my opponent around the constituency on campaigns. They went around telling my supporters that President Museveni didn't want me to win but he could not tell me so, and that was why he was sending this other candidate and seeking their support for her. I had even discussed the issue with the First Lady who told me that she had asked the woman to step down but she had refused. So I had decided to rely on my God as always and tussle it out with them. I had come face to face with treachery that I had never known before.

The next day in the morning, at around 9.00 a.m., as I was getting ready to leave for Ibanda County to start my campaigns, a delegation of men and women from my constituency in Buremba came to inquire as to what had happened between me and President Museveni. They were literally in tears. The people of Buremba, Kazo loved me so much because I was serving very well and they knew I supported President Museveni with all my heart. I had just been campaigning for him and he had won the elections. So they wanted to know what had gone wrong now that he had apparently sent Jovia Saleh with a delegation to move from place to place and tell people in the constituency that he did not want me any more and so they should not elect me but should elect Jovia Rwakishumba instead.

The group said that the people of Kazo could not believe it and so had asked them to come and find out from me what had gone wrong between me and the President. They wanted to know whether it was possible for them to reconcile us, if at all something had gone wrong. They added that they could not believe that after all my campaigning for Museveni, and knowing how committed to my work and to the government I was, that the President could have all of a sudden dumped me like that. It hurt them very much.

As I was telling them that there was nothing wrong that I knew of, my telephone rang and I picked the call. It was President Museveni on the line: "Matembe, how are you and how are you doing in the campaigns?"

"How am I doing in the campaigns? How can you ask me how I'm doing when you must know that I am not doing well since you are fighting me? Mzee, how could you really fight me after I have worked so hard on your campaign to get you to win the election? How can your people put a candidate to stand against me and pump in all this money so that she can defeat me? What and where did I go wrong to lose your support? When did I stop to be the favoured candidate for the Movement? Even right here before me are some of my supporters from Kazo who have come to ask me what happened between me and you that has caused you to fight me by sending them another candidate of your choice? Can a divided kingdom stand?" I was roaring. I had no time for protocol and decorum.

You see, I was so angered by what the people from Kazo had just said and was still disturbed by Kutesa's midnight conversation that words simply flowed out of my mouth in fury. Mark you, I was speaking in Runyankore.

After I had vented my frustration, the President replied, "Yes, Matembe, I have heard about that woman who is contesting against you; these people in the Movement told me that you have not been working hard in your constituency. That when you became a minister you became too busy for the constituency and abandoned your people, and so they are not ready to elect you but prefer another candidate. So these people in the Movement are worried that if we do not field another candidate, we will lose our seat to the opposition (the Reform Agenda). They said that instead of losing our seat by supporting you, we would rather support another candidate who will defeat the Reform Agenda candidate."

His response made me even more annoyed. "Who are these people in the Movement you are talking about whom you trust more than me? How can you believe that woman who you are fielding can be better than me, who has been your right-hand person in Mbarara District? If I have always won elections as an ordinary member of parliament, how can I lose now that I am a minister; you know very well that our people love having a minister as their MP? In any case, are you fielding candidates against other ministers? I am not the only minister. Mzee, this is a real conspiracy against me and it is hurting me deeply. If you did not want me, why did you not tell me early, before the nominations, so that I do not run, instead of sponsoring a candidate against me?"

He replied: "You see, I also did not think that you were going to lose until recently, when these people came to tell me."

"But why didn't you ask me if it were true instead of believing and siding with them?" I asked.

He replied, "You see, Matembe, you have a problem. When I tried to plead for you, I was asked how I could defend you and yet you were also fighting other colleagues."

"Which colleagues am I fighting?"

"You are fighting the censured ministers and the other officials such as Enos Tumusiime, who was involved in corruption charges with Uganda Railways. You told the electorate not to vote for them and so they are angry with you."

"But sir, what do you, yourself, think?" I asked. "Here we are being hailed for doing a good job fighting corruption by punishing the big fish and now you say I am doing wrong to appeal to the electorate not to vote for people involved in corruption? What would you say yourself, if you were asked by the public whether it were right to elect such people to parliament? Would you say, 'yes, it is good; go and elect them?' I thought I was doing a good job for you as your minister and I thought we were together in this fight. I did not know that my enthusiasm to work would bring me trouble from you and your people."

The President said, "But you see, these people are our strong cadres and they say I cannot defend you when you are fighting them." He went on to explain: "These censured ministers cannot be punished twice. They were punished by censure and they have already served their sentence. You, a lawyer, must be aware of the legal principle of double jeopardy. If these people have served their sentences by being censured out of cabinet, how can you now prevent people from electing them?"

I replied, "Sir, I do not understand you. I thought you and I were committed to fighting corruption and it would do us good when people tainted with corruption are not elected. I thought we would prefer people who have not been implicated in corruption scandals."

"Yes, I am with you in the fight against corruption, but I want you to know that it is not fair to punish people twice for the same offence and the law forbids it. Have you forgotten the law? For instance, look at this case of Tumusiime, how does it differ from Kazoora's case? Hon John Kazoora of Kashari was once prosecuted for a criminal offence, and after winning the case, he contested in elections, and even now he is contesting again. How is he different from Tumusiime who is now contesting in Makindye, and yet you have appealed to his electorate not to vote for him. Don't you see that you are fighting your colleagues?"

As I patiently listened to the President defending his corrupt allies, I understood what type of person I was dealing with. After our lengthy discussion, he requested me to write a letter to the Daily Monitor newspaper, which had published my statement, and say that it was alright for the censured ministers to be elected because they had served their sentence and therefore should not be punished twice. Further, since there were no criminal charges against them, there was nothing that prevented them from contesting in the elections.

I told the president that I could not do that because my conscience did not agree with it.

Then he said, "Matembe, I am asking you to kindly do this for me. Moreover, when you do it, I will ask that woman who is disturbing you to step down. Please write the letter now and send it to the Monitor, so that it is published tomorrow."

That ended our conversation. I am telling you, if I had ever been so depressed, so demoralized and so disheartened, during the time I had served in this Movement government, it was right then. That was when I came to the full realization that I was dealing with the wrong people. That was when I realized that the President was not at all interested in nor committed to fighting corruption. If he was, how could he blackmail me like that? How could he? There I was, having been nominated to run against a candidate fully backed by State House, and the President tells me that either I did what he wanted or I was finished, echoing the words of Kutesa, his in-law. In a nutshell, the President was saying, scratch my back and I scratch yours.

It was such a terrible morning for me and yet I was just about to go out to start my campaigns. It was so depressing. I asked myself, now what do I do? This is the President of the country saying, kindly do this for me. Who am I to put my foot down and say no way? I felt so abused, vulnerable, so miserable and extremely helpless. It was extremely disheartening, but obediently, I wrote the letter as he had told me to. I rang the Daily Monitor newspaper and asked them to publish the letter without fail otherwise I was finished. The letter was published the next day. But from that time onwards, I lost my faith and trust in the system I was working in; it was such a rude re-awakening.

After my first campaign rally in Ibanda, someone came to me and said, "You know, Hon Matembe, this candidate who is contesting against you, Jovia Rwakishumba, has no qualifications; she is using the certificates of a certain teacher called Kyomugisha who is a teacher at Kako SS in Masaka." He added that if I gave him some money for transport, he would go to Kako SS and verify this for me because he knew the teacher. I gave the man the money to travel to Kako to find out the truth. I also rang my lawyer in Kampala and instructed him to go and ask Kyomugisha if she had given her certificates to Rwakishumba. Luckily, this man from Ibanda met my lawyer at Kako, and together they confronted Kyomugisha about the forged papers. Kyomugisha denied giving her papers to Rwakishumba. She said Rwakishumba had taken her documents without her consent. She also said that it was true that Rwakishumba did not have the required Advanced Level certificate qualifications. The two men came back and told me, and when I was about to go to the radio to announce my findings, I heard that she had stepped down.

I need to show the extent of the wickedness of the people I was dealing with. Believe it or not, these State House people tried to convince the opposition Reform Agenda candidate, Mary Frances Kabatereine, who was contesting against us, to step down so that I would remain in the race with Rwakishumba alone. The Movement's strategy was that if there was a Reform Agenda candidate competing in a constituency, then the Movement would have only one candidate to compete against that Reform Agenda candidate.

However, if the Movement had two candidates standing in that same constituency, then the weaker one would be persuaded to step down for the stronger one. If there was no candidate from the opposition, then all the Movement candidates could contest since it did not matter who won; they would all be from the Movement.

Now, because this treacherous Movement camp knew I was the stronger Movement candidate in my constituency, and yet they did not want me, rather than persuade Rwakishumba to step down, they tried to persuade the Reform Agenda candidate to step down! Their idea was, when the two of us in the Movement remained standing, it would not be necessary for Rwakishumba to step down; instead, they would support her with all their money to defeat me. I was told that they invited the Reform Agenda candidate to State House to persuade her to step down by offering her money but she refused. She was so angry with them for betraying me.

When that plan failed, they tried to trap me into 'buying' Rwakishumba out of the race. Before the nomination day, Mrs Jovia Saleh called me to Agip Motel in Mbarara to discuss what was happening; how Rwakishumba was disturbing my candidature. I told her that I thought I was doing well and was capable of defeating her even if she did not leave the race voluntarily. Jovia said, "But you never know with these elections, you can't tell, you might lose; now what about paying her to drop out of the race?"

I said, "Me, paying for what? I don't even have money for the campaign. And besides why should my money go for nothing? If she thinks she can defeat me, let her go on and defeat me. In any case, if she defeats me then the people of Mbarara don't want me, and therefore, why should I be selling myself to them?"

She said, "But what if we can raise this money for you so that she comes out?"

I said, "You know, if you want to raise money on your own accord to use it to convince her to come out that is your concern, but for me, I have nothing to do with that. I will pray to my God as I usually do."

Can you imagine that two days later, this same Jovia was the very woman leading the team of State House operatives and some of President Museveni's confidants in Mbarara that accompanied Jovia Rwakishumba for nomination? You can imagine the shock I got! When I was talking with Mrs Saleh, I thought she was on my side and interested in my winning. That's when I thanked my God who gave me the integrity I have. Imagine, if I was a person who craves for power, I would have accepted the deal to pay out Rwakishumba and would have been trapped so that everybody would have said, where is her integrity and what moral right does she have to fight corruption. I am now sure they were laying a trap for me so that they could put me in the press and portray me as a person of no integrity. But you know, when God is on your side, nobody can be against you. My God protected me from their evil schemes.

It was during the 2001 parliamentary elections that I came to know that I was dealing with treacherous people of no integrity. That is the time I came face to face with wickedness, dishonesty and deceit. It really killed my spirit because by nature, I depend so much on trust. I have this genuine naïve trust, and once I trust you, I can't imagine that you can be so wicked as to stab me in the back. The Movement politics taught me a lesson. That's when I came to the realization that I was not a politician, but a political worker, because real politicians do not have the kind of naïve trust I have that can lead you into real danger. And again, I remembered that even Jesus never entrusted His life to anybody because He knew human beings are potentially evil.

Later, when I pondered deeply as to why this State House camp was fighting me when I was a supporter, I concluded that it certainly had something to do with the issue of the presidential term limits. I believe the President knew I was against the removal of the presidential term limits from the Constitution because we had talked about it. He also knew that Hon Kazoora and Hon Bernadette Bigirwa, and in fact most of the MPs from Ankole would not support it. So the scheme was to make sure that people opposed to the impending amendment to remove the term limits were eliminated from parliament so that the amendment would not face the challenge it faced when they failed to defeat us. They chose to sponsor very weak people who would not have the backbone to oppose their schemes. Either way, this kind of treachery was too much for me and it killed my love for the Movement and its leadership.

# Chapter Five

# 2001 Elections: The Unleashing of Terror

## Violent Crackdown and Arrests in Mbarara Municipality on 'Orders from Above'

Both presidential and parliamentary elections of 2001 were characterized by massive violence, vote rigging and vote buying because for the first time since the NRM government came to power, President Museveni was being challenged by a colleague from within the Movement. The previous elections had been a walk-over for Museveni since he was competing with candidates from parties that were not a serious challenge due to the diminishing credibility of the old traditional parties.

The contest between Museveni and Besigye was bound to divide the Movement and so President Museveni felt that his chances of winning were highly threatened. Since he was not sure of smoothly sailing through as he had done before, the government deployed security operatives to unleash violence on the members of opposition across the whole country, especially against the supporters of Dr Besigye's Reform Agenda.

The worst violence, which resulted in the death of some people with many others injured and maimed, was in Rukungiri, the home district of Dr Kizza Besigye. There was heavy military deployment of the Presidential Protection Unit (PPU). Beatings and torture were recorded, and at least one death of Johnson Baronda who was reportedly shot to death by the PPU in March 2001.

Unfortunately, Mbarara, the district I represented in parliament and which overwhelmingly supported Museveni, also had its fair share of violence because Hon Winnie Byanyima, Dr Kizza Besigye's wife, was contesting for the parliamentary seat for Mbarara Municipality. She had supported her husband against Museveni in the presidential elections, and so there was no way the government, which now considered her an enemy, would let her win her seat back now that she was in the opposition. Therefore, as the parliamentary elections went into high gear, terror was unleashed against Hon Byanyima, her relatives, friends and her campaign team.

I had my share of persecution from the very people I had campaigned for to win the presidential elections, as I have already shown, but by the grace of God, I had won the parliamentary elections for Mbarara District Woman Representative. So then I found myself at war with the State House camp once again. This time it was because I decided to support Hon Winnie Byanyima's campaign for the Mbarara Municipality seat.

What was so painful, and indeed contributed to my reasons for fighting Hon Byanyima's war was that the people who were fighting me, despite my support for them, were the very people fighting Hon Byanyima who had in fact opposed them. As mentioned before, this Movement camp had not fought only me, they also campaigned against Hon Bernadette Bigirwa (RIP) and Hon Kazoora, both of whom had supported and campaigned for President Museveni. It did not make sense to me that the very government we supported fought us as vehemently as it fought its real opponents.

Hon Byanyima was a very popular member of parliament for Mbarara Municipality. Until Besigye stood against Museveni, Hon Byanyima and all of us mentioned above were on the same campaign team in support of Museveni. But now that she had turned against the government, the Movement did not want her to retain her seat.

Mr Ngoma Ngime, who was by then the RDC of Mbarara, was the preferred Movement candidate because they thought he was strong enough to unseat Hon Byanyima. However, Byanyima had two main advantages against Ngoma Ngime: one, she was very popular among the women who were the majority voters. Secondly, she was born and bred in Mbarara, as opposed to her opponent, who was from a different region altogether and was viewed as a 'foreigner'. So the government decided to resort to intimidation and harassment of the voters, rigging and vote buying, which made the whole political environment in Mbarara insecure and miserable.

At that time, I had just won my seat against Mary Kabatereine, the Reform Agenda candidate who, of course, had been supported by Hon Byanyima.

One bright Sunday morning when I was getting ready to go to church, I received a call. "Is that the Minister for Ethics and Integrity?"

"Yes," I replied.

"How can you, the Minister for Ethics and Integrity, let Mbarara go on fire; what are you doing?"

"May I know who is calling and what the problem is?" I asked.

"Never mind who I am. I have called to inform you, in case you do not know, that Mbarara is on fire. Innocent people are being rounded up and arrested, beaten and harassed, and some are already in police cells," the male voice said. "Among those arrested are the women from the Forum for Women in Democracy (FOWODE) who had come to observe the parliamentary elections in Mbarara. Many people are being thrown into police cells, including Winnie Byanyima's sisters. People are out there crying for help and what are you doing? You, as the Minister for Ethics and Integrity?" The caller added before hanging up.

I was so confused because I did not expect the kind of things the caller was telling me. We had just been celebrating our victory and were waiting for the next round of parliamentary elections for the mainstream constituencies that were due in a week's time. Little did we know that the terror that had been unleashed on other districts against the opposition had now descended upon us in Mbarara because there was a strong opposition candidate there. At that time I was staying with my friend, Jolly Mugisha, and other women friends who had campaigned with us. I told them about the caller and his message and we agreed that I should go to the police to verify this information.

I dressed up quickly and went to the district police station. What I found there was appalling, to say the least. So many people had their arms tied behind their backs and were being led to police cells while their friends and relatives followed them crying. As soon as I got out of my car, these people yelled and called out to me: "Now Honourable, do you see what you are doing to us? After we have voted for you and the President, we are now being tortured simply because we support our Winnie? You are so cruel! After using us to put you into power, you are now paying us back by imprisoning us!"

I recognized many of these people as they were the same ones we had campaigned with for President Museveni. In fact, many of them had also been my own agents who campaigned and worked for me to win my race for the woman seat.

I could not understand what was happening. I told them to take heart and keep calm as I went to the office to find out what the problem was. I found the district police commander in the office; he too was confused and depressed. I asked him what was happening, why he was arresting people. The man broke down in tears and said, "You Honourable! Have you also come to harass me? I have already had enough, I can't take it anymore."

I actually sympathized with him. Imagine, a man in charge of the district's security had broken down and was crying before his juniors and the public because he was frustrated, overwhelmed, and helpless! His authority had been undermined.

He said to me, "Hon Matembe, I cannot understand what you are doing to me. Everybody is ordering me left, right and centre to lock people up without telling me why. People are just brought and dumped here with orders that I must put them in police cells, and yet I do not know what they are charged with. All I am told is: 'orders from above'."

I asked him who was bringing these people to be jailed. He said it was state operatives and people from the intelligence office.

Fortunately as we were still talking, another lorry arrived with more people who had supposedly been arrested. A man following the lorry in a small car came out quickly and started slapping some of the people on the lorry as he shouted at them to come down. I got out of the office and ordered him to stop what he was doing. I had always seen that young man in Mbarara but I didn't know what his job was.

I asked him, "What are you doing and who are you to torture people like that and violate their human rights?"

He said he was from the intelligence office and he was arresting these people because they had abused the name of the President.

I asked him, "What offence is that in the Uganda Penal Code Act and who gave you the authority to do this?"

He said, "It is none of your business. I am following 'orders from above'."

By that time, President Museveni had been in power for 15 years and yet I had not seen or heard of anybody being arrested for such an offence as 'the abuse of the name of the President'. The President had been attacked many times in the media, whether print or electronic, and in public debates and other public fora, but nobody had ever been arrested for that. This seemed to be a new chapter in the era of Museveni's leadership.

Things were going too far. I told the district police commander to refuse to lock these people in the cells, and then I told the 'state operative' to stop what he was doing until I found out what was going on from the powers 'above'. The district police commander said he was scared that if he did not take this man's order, he would be arrested himself. This statement was so horrible; it reminded me of Amin's and Obote's times when it seemed as if anybody anywhere had the authority to arrest and torture people and even kill them or make them 'disappear' supposedly on 'orders from above'.

There already had been media reports about how some people in Rukungiri, Mbale and Kiboga had been tortured and others even killed in the just concluded presidential and district women parliamentary elections. I was alarmed that people might also be killed in Mbarara, which would be a big shame since both the President and I, the Minister for Ethics and Integrity, were from Mbarara. This nonsense had to stop. I decided to call the President and tell him what was going on and to find out whether it was with his knowledge, since this state operative had no respect for me, a government minister, who moreover had just been re-elected to parliament.

Hon Amelia Kyambadde, who was at that time the President's Principal Private Secretary, answered my call and told me that he was on a flight to Kasese District. Never the less, I explained to her what was happening in Mbarara and told her that I wanted to know whether State House was responsible for the chaos since apparently state operatives said they were acting on orders from above. She promised she would inform the President when he arrived in Kasese.

I decided to ring Salim Saleh, the President's brother, and luckily I got through to him and explained the chaotic situation in Mbarara. I told him I could not tolerate what was going on and that it was a big shame to mistreat people who had worked so hard to elect the President simply because now they supported Hon Winnie Byanyima. I added that, in a democracy, citizens have a right to vote for the person of their choice and it was not a crime for the people of Mbarara to support Hon Byanyima if she was serving them well.

He asked me to give the phone to the district police commander so that he could tell him the whole story, which he did. After a little while, Saleh called me back and said that he had ordered 'the state operatives' to stop arresting people and to release those they had arrested.

By that time, the District Chief Administrative Officer (CAO) Hezel Kafureka, had arrived at the police station, and he too was very angry at the chaos created in his district. Mr Kafureka and I told the district police commander that he was now safe to release those he had arrested and that he must refuse to arrest any more people since Saleh, also one of those 'powers from above', would protect him from arrest by those 'state operatives'.

## Convincing Hon Winnie Byanyima Not to Quit the Parliamentary Race

I left the police station as the detainees were being released. Since they included the women from FOWODE and Hon Winnie Byanyima's sisters, I decided to pass by her house to see whether she was safe. I found her at her home and she had just called a press conference to announce that she was withdrawing from the race since it was becoming too dangerous for her, her family and her supporters in the constituency and elsewhere in the country. She told me that the pressure and harassment they were facing was too much; it was not worth the effort. She had therefore deemed it prudent to step down. She said that what had happened to them in Rukungiri and other areas was already too much, and she was not ready to see the same happen in Mbarara.

I told her that we had already secured the release of her

sisters and other supporters and so it was not necessary for her to step down.

"Miria, I am scared for my life and the lives of all these people. Our government has become so cruel; anything can happen to us," Hon Byanyima said.

When I assured her that I was going to make sure that the political tension in Mbarara eased down, she laughed at me and told me that I did not understand the type of people I was dealing with. She said that she admired my naïve trust of these people but she was not sure I would manage the situation.

I replied, "For that matter, we could put everything to God."

She laughed again and said, "Miria, do you think that where these things have reached God can manage?"

I replied "Then this is the right time for God to intervene, because God starts where human effort ends."

Just as I was about to convince her not to address the press, her women agents from the polling stations where voter registration cards were being distributed came into the house crying. Some of them were injured, others had their blouses torn. One of them did not have her shoes. They narrated their ordeal to us. They told us that trucks had been transporting young boys and girls from Kanyaryeru Secondary School and other surrounding secondary schools to come and receive voters' cards from Mbarara Municipality. When Hon Byanyima's agents objected to that, they were beaten and chased away by some apparent state operatives.

This made matters worse and gave Hon Byanyima more reason to step down. "You see? They are giving cards to all these young people so that they can artificially boost the number of those who will vote against me. How can I continue in the race when the elections are already rigged?" she asked.

I told her I was going to deal with that too. Surely, it was downright wrong for the Electoral Commission to be issuing voter cards at that time, when the elections were just two days away. So I telephoned the Electoral Commission in Mbarara and told them that what they were doing was wrong and that they should stop their exercise.

By the time I left Winnie's home, I had convinced her to continue in the race. She addressed the press and then we prayed together and left everything to God.

Believing in God's intervention then, more than ever, I decided to proceed to the All Saints Church in Mbarara for the Sunday service. I pondered on these matters on the way to church and was amazed at how God can unite people who were opposed to each other. As I already mentioned, Winnie had supported the opponent I had just defeated, and as a matter of fact, she had always sponsored candidates against me even when we were both in the Movement. And yet here I was fighting for her when I should have been one of those opposing her! However, my faith tells me to love those who persecute us because in so doing we heap burning coals on them. Secondly, my commitment to gender equality and women's empowerment cannot allow me to persecute a fellow woman. Most importantly, why should anyone be persecuted for exercising his or her right to vote for a candidate of their choice?

I arrived at church when the service was about to end. All the same, I asked for an opportunity to address the congregation and told them what had been happening in town and all that we had been through. I condemned the intimidation and violence unleashed on innocent people and called upon the congregation to also shun it and refuse to participate in it. I asked the congregation to lift up the nation, and our town especially, to God because we urgently needed His grace and intervention if we were to go through the elections safely.

I later came to learn that supporters of Hon John Kazoora in Kashaari had also been tortured and intimidated, although not as fiercely as in the municipality.

## General Katumba Wamala Saves Us from Kakooza Mutale's infamous Kalangala Action Plan (KAP)

At around 3pm that same day, when things had calmed down, Major Kakooza Mutale arrived with his infamous Kalangala Action Plan (KAP), which had been accused of terrorizing people opposed to President Museveni in other districts. Kalangala Action Plan was a paramilitary group of NRM vigilantes under the command of Major Kakooza Mutale. The group, which was usually active during general elections, was infamous for harassing, intimidating and torturing citizens who did not support Museveni or any of his preferred candidates. *(Kakooza Mutale is, at the time of writing this book, a Senior Presidential Advisor on Political Affairs.)* Now that the Movement had an 'enemy' in the municipality in the name of Hon Winnie Byanyima, the political 'terrorists' had come to do their job. I resolved, there and then, to ensure that this group got out of Mbarara because I had heard about the havoc it caused wherever it went.

This time I telephoned General Katumba Wamala, then the Inspector General of Police. I told him all that we had already gone through and requested him to please order Kakooza Mutale out of our district. I remember telling him: "I know Kakooza Mutale is the President's man, but since in the army hierarchy you are a major general and he is only a major, if you order him to leave our district in peace, I am sure he will leave."

I am so grateful to Katumba Wamala because indeed he ordered the 'terrorist' out of our town. Kakooza Mutale had just taken over the High Street with his gang when all of a sudden, we saw his gang climb into a yellow bus and drive back out of town.

Within about 30 minutes of their departure, General Katumba Wamala called me to ascertain whether they had left. I remember thanking him for having rescued us from a man who was compared to one of Idi Amin's most notorious henchmen called Juma 'No Parking', nicknamed 'Butabika'(after the mental asylum in Kampala because of how he terrorized people).

When I eventually returned to Kampala and again thanked Katumba for rescuing us from the terror of Kakooza Mutale, he laughed and agreed with me, saying that indeed the man was 'No Parking' because when he left Mbarara that afternoon, he drove all the way, straight through Kampala, to Mbale where he unleashed his terror on the people there. As a matter of fact, the violence in Mbale and other Eastern districts resulted in some deaths.

It was reported that on 26th February 2001, during President Museveni's visit to Tororo and Busia, several people waved the victory sign to show their support for Dr Besigye as Museveni's team passed by. They were whisked on to the Movement's yellow bus that was under the command of Kakooza Mutale. Some were taken to police after they were thoroughly beaten. Isaac Katerega, one of the people who was flogged, was rushed to a hospital in Busia on the Kenyan side where he reportedly died from injuries afflicted by Kakooza Mutale's henchmen.

## Did President Museveni Abet the Electoral Violence in Mbarara Municipality?

That same Sunday evening, at about 8pm, I received a telephone call from President Museveni. He congratulated me upon winning my seat and asked me how the elections had gone. I told him it was good that he had called because I had been trying to reach him since morning to tell him about the violence that was taking place in Mbarara supposedly on orders 'from above'.

I told him that Hon Winnie Byanyima's sisters, her friends and agents had been harassed, arrested and thrown into prison, and the town had been in chaos. I asked him whether the orders were from him or any other lawful authority. He asked me what I did when I did not get him. I replied that I called Salim Saleh who told those who had been arresting innocent people to stop and release all those who had been detained.

I also told him I asked Katumba Wamala to recall Kakooza Mutale who had come to disturb our district, which he did, and that the town was now peaceful.

I went on to ask the President why there should be turmoil in our district simply because Hon Byanyima was contesting for a Parliamentary seat. I said, "Your Excellency, Hon Byanyima is just one person and all other members of parliament in the district are your supporters. What does it matter if Winnie retains her seat? Is there any need to harass your supporters who voted for you just because they like Hon Byanyima as well? Is it worth it to harass her and arrest her sisters and attract press reports that will undermine the electoral process?"

I suggested to him that Hon Byanyima should be left alone to go through her campaigns smoothly so that the people of Mbarara are left in peace. If she won, it would be no big deal; if she lost, at least she would have no reason to complain because she would have lost through a free and fair election. But with the violence, even if she was to genuinely lose, she would have the excuse that she would have won had it not been for the harassment and intimidation of voters.

After listening to me, his response was, "You see, Matembe, I received a call this morning saying that you are interfering in the work of the Electoral Commission. So I have called to ask why you are doing this. This is not your responsibility." He sounded very harsh and rude.

"What?" I exclaimed. "I am really shocked. I have been working so hard to save your home district from the chaos it was degenerating into, and your people are once again telling you lies about me?"I agreed that I had intervened in the work of the police by stopping them from co-operating with the 'state operatives' in harassing and imprisoning people.

"Yes, I did this because, as a responsible government minister, I did not want to see Mbarara on fire. I did not want to see people dying when you, the President, and I, your minister for Ethics and Integrity, come from Mbarara. Sir, how could I let the very people who had worked so hard for your success and mine be dumped in jail while their relatives were shouting and calling out to me for help?" I asked.

"As your Minister for Ethics and Integrity, I could not allow such unethical conduct by people calling themselves state operatives and yet they could not even respect a cabinet minister. Sir, you gave me a job, and I can never hesitate to do it at any time. If I had got you on phone, I would have taken your instructions. I did the responsible thing I was supposed to do."

I was so disappointed because I had expected appreciation from the President for a job well done now that the town was calm.

I added, "Your Excellency, it is not worth it to have violence. You have already won the elections, and some of us also have already won, and many more of your supporters will win too, and so it does not matter if Hon Byanyima wins. She is an MP who is very popular in her constituency. If the people who love you also love her, why should they be harassed and tortured for supporting her?"

"After all, they voted for you against Besigye and they deserve to be treated well. As for me, I stood for what is right and just. I cannot let wrong things happen, especially not in my constituency," I added.

"So sir, even if those people whom you trust more than me have continued to tell you lies, my God will exonerate me one day. After all, God has already shamed them by enabling me to win elections when they had deceived you that I was not wanted in the constituency. So what happens now that I won?" I asked.

After I had poured out my heart, he replied, softly this time, "Okay, Matembe, do not worry about the lies. It's good you helped to stop the chaos. It's alright. Continue doing your job and take heart." He wished me a good night and I did the same.

The truth is that, I did order the Electoral Commission to close up their office and stop issuing voters' cards because it was wrong. But when I detected anger in the President's voice, I concluded that he must have been in agreement with what the Electoral Commission was doing, and I did not want to indulge in that argument. I thought it was safer and better to concentrate on the issue of violence which had affected all these people who had voted for us. That way I hoped to get him to sympathize with them and thank me for helping them. I was so passionate as I talked that he dropped the issue of the interference with the work of the Electoral Commission and even softened his voice as he thanked and comforted me.

Finally, when the elections were held, both Hon Winnie Byanyima and Hon John Kazoora won their seats back against the NRM government wishes. However, from that time onwards, the Movement was never the same again because there was a big rift between those who were considered more loyal to the President and those who had been persecuted by the government despite the fact that they were Movement members who had supported President Museveni against Dr Kizza Besigye.

## The Movement of "We" and "They"

The NRM, which was supposed to accept everybody, now had 'we' and 'they'. NRM was clearly behaving like a party even though we had not returned to a multiparty political system. It is true that some of the Movement people had supported Besigye's presidency bid against Museveni. But that was not an offence since the Constitution permitted anybody to contest for any position, including the presidency, provided he or she had the qualifications to do so. Hon Byanyima belonged to the Movement as much as any one of us did, despite the fact that she had campaigned for and supported her husband against Museveni.

What crime had she committed? What was a wife expected to do, abandon her husband? In any case Besigye had lost the presidential elections, so what was the big deal?

In democratic governance, if a candidate loses during the party primaries, aren't his or her supporters supposed to support the winner at the national level for the good of the party? This was not the case with the Movement politics. The leadership of the Movement viewed all those who had either supported or sympathized with Dr Kizza Besigye as enemies of not only the government but the country as a whole. Even when the Movement became a political party, it sustained the view that whoever disagrees with President Museveni is an enemy of the party, and the country too, who must be fought by the party and the government machinery. This has been seen most recently in the fallout between President Museveni and his former close ally and Prime Minister, John Patrick Amama Mbabazi, after the latter expressed his intentions in 2015 to stand against Museveni as the Party President and Head of State. Such ostracism is extremely unfortunate for our country.

In fact, after the elections of 2001, some people had to flee the country, including Dr Kizza Besigye himself. Even Hon Winnie Byanyima, despite winning her seat, never had the peace and opportunity to occupy it because the harassment and intimidation by police continued, until she too probably thought it was not worth it for her to stay around to enjoy her term of office in parliament and her constituency. She too left the country.

Incidentally, I too had to pay my share for the 'sin' of assisting her to win because that placed me in the category of the 'enemies' of the Movement and the government. I actually think I had already been placed in that category, and my supposed assistance to Hon Winnie Byanyima was simply an excuse. Otherwise why had the State House camp sponsored Rwakishumba against me when they knew of my total commitment and service to the Movement government and the country?

By the end of the 2001 parliamentary elections, I concluded that the President, his family and his closest allies had an agenda, unknown to the rest of us who were considered enemies. Otherwise why had they fought us and regarded us as enemies when we were not?

I was told that my problem was my support for Hon John Kazoora. If only I could disown him then I would be a good girl. However, I saw no reason for not supporting Kazoora, a man who had gone to the bush even before his university graduation to join Museveni and fight for the freedom of the country. Hon Kazoora is, in fact, my uncle although he is younger than me by a few years. He is the young man who inspired me to join the Movement in 1986 when he arrived from the bush as a victorious freedom fighter and became the Special District Administrator (SDA) for Kampala District.

I have never known why the leadership of the Movement got to hate Hon Kazoora but they really hate the man. I remember, one time in cabinet when they were talking about him with such bitterness and calling him all sorts of names such as 'acidulous'. At some point I could not take it any longer and I burst out: "I now know you people want to kill Kazoora so that I may remain alone."

They were surprised by my remarks. One minister, I think it was Hon Edward Rugumayo asked, "Are they related?" and the President answered, "Yes, he is her cousin." That marked the end of the debate on Kazoora that day.

# Chapter Six

# The Aftermath of the 2001 General Elections

## The Parliamentary Swearing-in Ceremony Photo Drama

In 2001, after our attempts to convince Dr Besigye to drop his presidential bid had failed, we, the members of the Ankole caucus, with the single exception of Hon Winnie Byanyima, decided to support President Museveni against Besigye. So while we were all on the campaign team for Museveni, she alone was on her husband's team. Ironically, Hon John Kazoora, who had supported and campaigned for President Museveni, was as intensely persecuted as Hon Winnie Byanyima who had supported Besigye. The intense persecution they experienced from the government united them in their struggle.

During the swearing-in ceremony of members of parliament, whenever any member was called up to the front to be sworn in, his or her colleagues, friends and relatives accompanied him or her to the front. So when Hon Winnie Byanyima and I, together with others, were accompanying Hon Kazoora to the front, a certain cameraman calculatingly snapped Hon Byanyima and I in a very happy mood. Of course, it was a moment of excitement for us to celebrate John's success; he had given a heavy blow to the government forces that fought against him. The next day, the photograph was published in one of the dailies with the caption: *'Matembe accompanies Winnie for swearing-in'*. All this was calculatedly done to depict me as an enemy of the government since I was associating with the woman who had supported Besigye against Museveni.

That picture was not only misleading but a falsehood too. In the first place, I was not accompanying Hon Winnie Byanyima; I was accompanying Hon Kazoora. Secondly, assuming I was accompanying her, what was wrong with celebrating her victory since she was, in fact, still one of us in the Movement? However, all those people in the Movement leadership who had been fighting me thought they now had in their hands 'clear evidence' that supposedly incriminated me as an enemy of the state. The picture apparently portrayed me as a good friend of Hon Winnie Byanyima, who opposed Museveni, and therefore the government, so I could not be supporting it either. That was the false conclusion. I was 'a mere pretender'.

By this time, the politics of patronage, which had

instilled fear in Ugandans, was already at play. So the day the picture appeared in the press, many of my friends called me and expressed fear as to what I was going to do now that I had been portrayed as Hon Winnie Byanyima's ally. I told them I did not care whether the Movement leadership liked me or not, as long as my conscience was clear. Many members of parliament, whom I had worked with in support of President Museveni, started avoiding me whenever we met at the parliamentary canteen because they feared being labeled 'enemies of the government' by associating with me 'the traitor' simply because of that photograph with Hon  Winnie Byanyima.

I remember my good friend Hon Elly Karuhanga calling me and asking whether I had seen the picture in the papers. He wondered what I was going to do, especially about my relationship with Hon Janet Museveni, the First Lady. He said, "*Mbwenu reru munywani wangye, kawafa. Kawareeba. Ekishushani eki, notoorahi?* Meaning, I am sorry for you, my friend, what are you going to do about this photograph?

Incidentally, the First Lady and Hon Winnie Byanyima are not the best of friends because at one time President Museveni was widely rumoured-to have had an intimate relationship with Hon Winnie Byanyima. So how could I be the First Lady's friend and yet be close to Hon Winnie Byanyima? My apparent closeness to Hon Winnie Byanyima put my loyalty to the First Lady in question.

I told Hon Elly Karuhanga that I was surprised by people's malice, but since my conscience was clear and I knew I was not against the government, it did not matter what others thought. There wasn't much more I could do to prove my support for the government leadership if campaigning for the President was not good enough.

## A Revealing Encounter with Hon Sam Kutesa

Indeed, whoever took that photograph achieved their purpose because it created the desired outcome.

One evening after the swearing in ceremony, President Museveni hosted all the members of the outgoing 6th Parliament to dinner at the Nakasero State House. He wanted to thank us for the work we had done and bid us farewell since there was a new parliament. All the members of the 6th Parliament, including those who had retained their seats and those who had lost them, were invited to the dinner and given certificates of appreciation.

Regrettably, at that dinner, I had the misfortune of sharing a table with Hon Sam Kutesa. He came in with some other members, including Hon Hope Mwesigye and Hon Hanifa Kawoya. As soon as he sat at the table and saw me, he greeted me and then looked me straight in my eyes and said, "*Iwe mwinaziwe, mbwenushi katwarugaho tukakumanya. Reka ngu otaaha noyeshereka, mbwenu omushana tugukwanikire okahemuka? Turigireho twakumanya, nambwenu waza kutureeba ekiturakukore ihano we.*" In short, he said, "You wicked person. We now know your true colours. You have been pretending that you are for us, when you are an enemy. All things have now been brought to the light and surely you have been disgraced. You will see what we will do to you." As he said all this, he waved the newspaper with the photograph of Hon Winnie Byanyima and I.

He went on to say, *"Manya kubakugamba ogira ngu nibakubeherera mbwenu nekishushani kyakubeherera?"* Meaning, you have been saying that the press publishes lies about you; is this photograph a lie?

I responded by telling him that yet again, the press had misrepresented me because I had not accompanied Hon Winnie Byanyima, but rather Hon Winnie Byanyima and I were accompanying Hon John Kazoora. I knew, however, that what I was saying did not matter to him; what mattered was that they had 'proof' that I was a traitor since I was seen sharing a moment of joy with Hon Byanyima, an 'enemy'.

And did it really matter to him whether I was accompanying Hon John Kazoora or Hon Winnie Byanyima? They were both regarded as 'enemies'. Nonetheless, I thought I should put the record straight.

He reiterated his earlier statement, *"Oryomwinazi kandi okuruga hati noza kutureeba"* meaning, you are evil and from now onwards, you will have it rough with us.

I asked him what he was going to do to me.

"You are not going to get the job of a minister anymore," he said.

"Is that all?" I replied. "Do you think I am craving for that job? That job which has given me sleepless nights and exposed me to hatred? Do you really think that I have anything to lose by being relieved of that job? Do you think I enjoy it when all the sins of you, the corrupt, are heaped on me as if I were corrupt myself? If you did not know, I am already fed up with fighting corruption almost single-handedly without the support of the government."

I added that I was in fact praying that I would not be re-appointed to the cabinet. I would be very happy and satisfied to serve my country as a backbencher. I told him that if he thought not being re-appointed a minister was a punishment, he was wrong. It would be such a great relief to me.

He repeated his earlier statement that they would deal with me anyway.

The language Kutesa was using was very personal: 'We shall deal with you'; 'we have come to know you'; 'we won't re-appoint you'.

Who were 'we'? I asked myself. Him and who? Was Kutesa the appointing authority?

This language was very revealing to me, because it showed me who had the real authority in the country. The fact that he had been censured by parliament for corruption did not matter. He knew he had the power to handle the Minister for Ethics and Integrity who was responsible for fighting corruption. And, of course, the language he used reminded me of my earlier conversation with him before the elections, and the intervention of the President on his behalf, ordering me to withdraw my statement about the censured ministers. It made it clear to me who was who in Museveni's government. Some of those implicated in corruption scandals were not only more powerful now, but were trusted even more by the President. Such incidents left me in no doubt that President Museveni's government is a family affair. Hon Kutesa, as an in-law of the President, was as powerful as Salim Saleh, the President's brother.

Where then was my authority as a full cabinet minister of the government? I'm afraid that even now, the 'we' camp of the Movement still possesses more authority than cabinet ministers and other officials in similar positions of power.

Later, I would come to learn from my friend, the late Hon Bernadette Bigirwa, that Hon Sam Kutesa had approached her and said that they were fed up with me and did not want to re-appoint me as Minister for Ethics and Integrity. He told her that they wanted to appoint her as minister instead.

Hon Bernadette Bigirwa was not at all amused by Kutesa's message, which he had thought was going to excite her. Instead she told him, "You had been fighting both of us to prevent us from joining parliament, and now that we have defeated you, you want to divide us? If you want to give me a job, give me mine and not Matembe's, otherwise leave me alone."

"I am satisfied with being a member of parliament," she added. "In any case, who are you to give out jobs; are you the President?" she asked.

Hon Bernadette Bigirwa had been a member of the 6th Parliament that had censured Hon Sam Kutesa. It was so annoying for her to see someone who had been censured now posturing before her as the appointing authority with the power to appoint her a minister.

She told me all this much later, but unfortunately she died too early. I was very pleased with these two women of integrity, Hon Bernadette Bigirwa and Ms Mary Kabatereine, who refused to succumb to the wicked schemes of those who have excelled in the skill of divide and rule. I wish we could have more of such women leaders in our country. Sadly, they have become more scarce instead.

After all this, I realized that I had no place in the hearts of the Movement leadership; if anything they were just using me as a cover up for their corruption.

> *The Lord says: "These people come near to me with their mouth and honor me with their lips, but their hearts are far from me... (Isaiah 29:13)*

I came to the conclusion that President Museveni was not committed to fighting corruption, since his close relatives and confidantes were implicated in the malpractice and yet he preferred to work with them and to defend them. So it became clear to me that the ministry was just a cover up. I was a big mouth shouting that the government was committed to fighting corruption, and yet behind my back the contrary was happening. I started praying that I do not get re-appointed to the cabinet. My desire was to simply remain a backbencher where my role would be to critique the government rather than defend it and carry its sins on my back. I knew that I was not Jesus to carry the sins of the government.

## To Turn Down the Ministerial Appointment or Not?

A week after the general elections and my encounter with Hon Sam Kutesa, President Museveni announced his new cabinet, which included the censured ministers Hon Sam Kutesa and Hon Jim Muhwezi at full ministerial level. Major Kakooza Mutale, who had been terrorizing people with his Kalangala Action Plan during the elections, was appointed a minister of state. I was also re-appointed, but this time as a Minister of State. Imagine, the censured ministers had been promoted to full cabinet positions while I, the Minister for Ethics and Integrity, who had worked so hard to establish the ministry, and had prepared the government's action plan and strategy to fight corruption, was demoted from a full cabinet minister to a minister of state. So, I was accorded the same rank as Major Kakooza Mutale whom I had chased from Mbarara to prevent him from causing havoc in the municipality during the parliamentary elections. What an irony!

Incidentally, this pattern of rewarding wrongdoers while punishing those who do good has persisted up to the present day in Museveni's government, as evidenced by the 2010 cabinet reshuffle after the Temangalo corruption scandal that involved Hon Amama Mbabazi, who the president described as 'Mr Clean'. After his spirited fight for Hon Amama Mbabazi, the president reshuffled his cabinet and dropped those ministers who had not supported Hon Amama Mbabazi and appointed or promoted his supporters. The promoted ministers included Hon Hope Mwesigye, from Minister of State to full cabinet minister; Hon Kakooza to Minister of State; and Hon Perez Ahabwe to Minister of State.

All along I had thought that since they had been fighting me, and Kutesa had made it clear that they would deal with me, I was not going to be re-appointed. So, when my name was announced, I was not only surprised but also very disappointed. I did not wish to be re-appointed at all, and yet here I was in the same cabinet together with the men who had been censured for corruption during my first tenure of office. Besides, the President had already given presidential pardon to some of those we had successfully prosecuted for corruption, such as Hon Mulindwa Birimumaso.

Clearly the President's conduct was in contradiction to the work of my portfolio, and I genuinely felt that I would not be able to do much to fight corruption since the government was not at all committed to the fight. In any case, I was no longer interested in working with leaders who apparently did not want me, but were only using me to promote their own interests.

After hearing my name announced on the radio, I felt the urge to call a press conference and turn down the appointment. But being a believer in Jesus Christ, I remembered the Lord's command to us to respect those who are in authority. In President Museveni's government, ministerial appointees are publicly announced in the media, without first informing the individuals concerned, or consulting them to find out if they are willing to take on the job or not. It is therefore quite rude and embarrassing to the appointing authority to turn down the job offer after he has already made the announcement.

The first time I was appointed, I remember asking President Museveni why he appointed ministers without first consulting them. He gave me two reasons. He said that once you are a member of parliament you have already clearly expressed your interest in serving the nation, so it does not matter in which capacity you are requested to serve. Secondly, if he was to consult with the appointees first, people would know that there is going to be a cabinet reshuffle and he would be overwhelmed by politicians lobbying for ministerial positions.

I thought it would be disrespectful of me to call a press conference and publicly turn down the ministerial offer. I therefore sought an appointment with the President through his Principal Private Secretary, who at the time was Ms Hilda Musubire. I told her that I did not want the appointment and wanted to communicate my reasons to the President. When Musubire told the President, his response was that he was too busy to see me, but that he strongly advised me to take up the appointment. He went on to say that if I felt so strongly about turning down the job, I should communicate my decision to the parliamentary committee that approved presidential appointments.

I informed Musubire that I was not going to appear before the parliamentary committee, but I was going to call a press conference and explain publicly why I was turning down the offer. Within a few minutes she told me that the President wanted to see me immediately. I wondered where he had got the time to do so since he had earlier said he was too busy. I am sure he got worried as to what I was going to tell the public through the press, so, he opted to give me a hearing instead.

When I went to see him that evening, I found that indeed he was busy because he had organised a dinner for some people. I was also asked to join the diners and the program went on beyond midnight. After his guests had left, we had our meeting in the late hours of the night, and it went on up to around 3 a.m. We had a lengthy discussion in which I submitted my reasons for declining his offer.

First, I told the President that I did not think that he was committed to fighting corruption and therefore it would be useless for me to continue in this job, since he and I would be working at cross purposes. Of course, I discussed the issue of the censured ministers and reminded him of his order to retract my statement about them. I told him of the implications of their re-appointments, moreover on promotion, on the government's effort to fight corruption. I said that by the very fact of promoting the censured ministers and demoting the minister responsible for fighting corruption, he was signaling to both the public and the development partners that he was not committed to fighting corruption.

Secondly, I said that he had undermined the authority of the Ministry of Ethics and Integrity by demoting the portfolio, since a junior minister does not have the power to question the conduct of a full cabinet minister. As a full cabinet minister, I would have had the authority to call my fellow cabinet ministers and discuss queries of corruption and other unethical conduct that may have been raised against them or within their ministries. But protocol does not grant such authority to a junior cabinet minister of state.

Thirdly, I told him that I was not ready to work under the authority of any other minister, especially not under Hon Gilbert Bukenya, the appointed Minister, Office of the President, because he had been under investigation by the Office of the Inspector General of Government for corruption. How could the Minister for Ethics and Integrity be under the supervision of someone who had been strongly suspected of engagement in corrupt practices?

I must say that the President gave me a good hearing. In his response, among other things, he told me that when he made me a minister of state, his intention was to re-organize the Office of the President so that there was only one minister in charge of the presidency and the rest of the ministers in his office were then made ministers of state. He had not perceived it as a demotion. He said it had not been his intention to undermine the Ministry of Ethics and Integrity, and that he had not realized that making its head a junior minister had negative implications on his will to fight corruption.

The President said that it was nevertheless too late to remedy the situation because he had already announced all the ministers in the president's office as ministers of state, except the minister in charge of the presidency. Besides, he was limited by the Constitution on the number of ministries the government could have. As far as he was concerned, he said, he saw no practical difference between a minister and a minister of state, since each minister was responsible for a specific assignment within the ministry.

When I insisted that I was not ready to take up his job, he implored me to take it up, saying that he had nobody else to do this particular job for him. "Matembe, kindly help me, you have been doing this job so well, and I do not have anybody who can do it as well," he pleaded.

I replied, "If you knew I was doing it well, and you do not have anybody to do it as well, why have you demoted me? Is that how you reward those who do well, while promoting those implicated in corruption?"

*"Matembe nyaburawe, nsasira tinkudimotingire, ninkushaba ngu onyetegyereze onyambe."* Meaning, Matembe, please forgive me; I did not demote you. Kindly understand and help me.

I could understand the issue of re-organising the President's Office by making all six of us ministers who were by then in his office ministers of state in charge of different portfolios. I, however, could not understand the re-appointment, moreover on promotion, of the censured ministers and Major Kakooza Mutale. But I could not push this matter any further; this was His Excellency, the Head of State, after all. It was certainly too much for me to see him plead with me, and I realized it would not be respectful of me to insist on turning down the appointment. So, I decided to accept the appointment on two conditions: One, that I was not going to be answerable to the minister in charge of the presidency because that undermined my office, and two, I was going to do the job on my own terms.

He asked me, "What do you mean by doing the job on your own terms?"

"Sir," I replied, "when I see anything wrong, I will speak out irrespective of who is involved. I am not going to keep quiet about anybody involved in unethical or corrupt practices, and I am not going to yield to you to withdraw statements like you requested I do that time with the censured ministers. I must follow my conscience and will not be used as a shield to cover up the sins of others. I have no problem at all working as a backbencher in parliament because my freedom to express myself without being compromised and blackmailed is more important to me than this job."

To this he replied, "I see; if that is what you mean, then it's okay. Go do your work as you wish, and in doing your work, you are not answerable to anybody else except me. Is that okay?"

I told him I would be assured about my not being answerable to the minister in charge of the President's Office if he put it in writing because protocol demanded that a minister of state be answerable to the full cabinet minister. He assured me that he was going to do that, and indeed he wrote the letter informing the cabinet that for practical purposes, all the ministers of state in the Office of the President were full cabinet ministers who were entitled to attend cabinet meetings in their own right and were directly answerable to him.

So, after agreeing with these terms, I accepted to take on the job. However, my term of office was cut short because one and half years down the road, I opposed Museveni's bid to remove the presidential term limits of two terms from the Constitution and he dropped me from the cabinet. I say he 'dropped' me but others say he sacked me. In my view, one is sacked for inefficiency or any other kind of misconduct. But in my case, I was dropped for being committed to and enthusiastic about doing my job well. Little did I know that I was not meant to do my job, but rather, to use the office to cover up wrong-doing!

# Chapter Seven

## Kyankwanzi – The Theatre of Uganda's Political Tragedy

### The Removal of the Presidential Term Limit and Politics of 'Kisanja'

Due to the strange manner in which things were unveiling themselves in the governance of the country after the 2001 elections, many people started expressing concern as to whether President Museveni would relinquish power in 2006. The term ending in 2006 would be his second and last one since the Constitution provided a maximum of two presidential terms. It would also mean that Museveni would have been in power for twenty years, making him the longest-serving president in Uganda's history.

As skepticism about President Museveni's willingness to peacefully handover power in 2006 grew, media houses and journalists started asking him what he was going to do. To this question, he would say that he would follow the Constitution. On one of his international visits, he was asked this question during an interview with the BBC. As usual he cunningly responded that, "I will follow the Constitution."

This evasive response to the BBC raised doubts in my mind and I started thinking like some people who were sure that he would not leave power. Because of my legal background, I kept wondering why, if Museveni was ready to hand over power, he didn't categorically say so? That is when it dawned on me that he would change the Constitution by scrapping the provision of term limits and then tell people that he was following the Constitution.

My fears came to pass in 2003 during the meeting of the National Executive Committee of NRM at Kyankwanzi when he revealed his plan to us.

In the early years of the NRM rule, Kyankwanzi had become the Mecca of Uganda's politics. It is an important historic place because it was the epicentre of the five-year-long guerrilla war that brought NRA into power. With such historical symbolism, it is no wonder that it became the de-facto headquarters of the NRM political ideology; an arena for debate and free exchange of ideas within the Movement. Many young people and civil servants were schooled there in the NRM philosophy during short political courses known as *Mchaka Mchaka*. It was ironic that this historic place where the progressive and democratic ideals of the Movement were taught was later to play host to one of the most flagrant anti-constitutional manoeuvres in Uganda's history.

It was at Kyankwanzi that Museveni introduced his bid to remove the presidential term limits. Personally, I was vehemently opposed to this move, first as a lawyer but also as a patriotic Ugandan. I had been a member of the Uganda Constitutional Commission that had collected people's views, on the basis of which we made a draft constitution. I had traversed the whole country and knew the sentiments and views of the people of Uganda on the issue of term limits. It was the people of Uganda who had proposed it. Therefore, there was no way I was going to betray the people by participating in the removal of the term limits.

Ugandans had hoped and believed that term limits would provide checks and balances against dictatorship, and now here was another dictator in-the-making who did not want to leave power. The people of Uganda had perceived the presidential term limits as the only way to peacefully change power from one president to another. This proposal in the draft constitution was overwhelmingly endorsed by the Constituent Assembly to which I was also a delegate. How then could I support its removal? And even more so that I was now the Minister for Ethics and Integrity? How could I in good conscience endorse its removal? I had to act ethically and with integrity.

So, of course, I angered the President so much. His confidants thought I had gone beyond the limit when I openly opposed his bid, even though the majority of the people there supported him. In my presentation at Kyankwanzi, I told him, "Your Excellency, you went to the bush to fight Obote because he had rigged the elections. But you are now doing the same. The election violence which you went to the bush to fight against was carried out to the maximum against those opposed to your presidency in the last elections."

I also told him that his government had become very corrupt,and yet one of the points of the Movement's Ten-Point Program was to fight corruption. I went on to tell him that his proposal to remove the constitutional presidential term limits was a form of corruption, and as his minister in charge of fighting corruption, I was not prepared to support him.

Though I was not surprised by his bid, it still shocked me. It totally shattered my faith, trust and hope in President Museveni. That is why I did not mince my words in telling him my mind. For me, this was the point of no return.

At this critical yet tragic NEC meeting in Kyankwanzi, three other key members of the NRM opposed his bid to remove the term limits. They were: General Mugisha Muntu,the former Army Commander; Hon Mathew Rukikaire, a former minister and historical member of the Movement; and Hon Bidandi Ssali, a veteran politician and also a historical member of the Movement, who was at that time the Minister for Local Government.

After the Kyankwanzi conference, the resolution to remove the constitutional presidential term limits was within a week passed by the National Conference at the International Conference Centre in Kampala.

## Aftermath of the Kyankwanzi Resolution to Remove the Presidential Term Limit

About two weeks after the National Conference had endorsed the Kyankwanzi Resolution, Museveni invited members of the Ankole parliamentary caucus for a meeting at his country home in Rwakitura. This is his practice when he wants to coerce members opposed to his ideas; he simply invites people without informing them of the purpose of the meeting. So when we reached his home, we found that he had called us to grill us as to why we, the Banyankore, were determined to make him fail by sabotaging his government. He told us that MPs from other regions had told him that we were the ones sabotaging his government.

You can imagine us hearing such a statement coming from the President, whom we had resolved to support, and indeed supported as a bloc when he stood against Dr Kizza Besigye in the presidential elections. Yes, it is true, as l have already mentioned, that we had all along noted and discussed with the President the weaknesses in the government which Dr Besigye had also written about in his dossier. But we had nevertheless gone ahead to support Museveni, hoping that after the elections we would be able to clean, re-organize, and re-direct the Movement government back to the original ideals for which it had come to power. But to our shock, he instead came up with this bid, which in effect was for a life presidency. Such a bid could not of course go down well with the majority of us in the Ankole parliamentary caucus.

However, apart from some of us publicly opposing

the removal of the term limits, none of us had done anything to sabotage his government. We were therefore not at all pleased by his accusations. He insisted that we were undermining him and presented to us a document containing the issues we were supposed to discuss.

In this document he specifically singled out Hon John Kazoora, Hon Guma Gumisiriza and I as problematic.

"Look at people like this Matembe, who is the Minister for Ethics and Integrity! Look at what she did at Kyankwanzi; publicly opposing the removal of the term limits. What kind of minister is this?" The President roared angrily.

Once again, I was shocked by the President's remarks because I had, all along, not thought that I had done anything wrong since I had expressed my sincere views on the issue. I, genuinely, believed in the retention of the presidential term limits because it was the only safety net for us as Ugandans, against a historical background of former presidents who had refused to relinquish power peacefully; a factor that had caused us untold suffering. I was simply doing my duty as a citizen.

He went on to say, however, that I talked at a wrong forum. "You should not have talked like that to those ignorant people. How can you talk about such important issues of government to people like the chairmen of LC III and LCV? A minister should not discuss such issues at a forum of lower-level people like that."

He went on and on. I could not believe my ears as the President called the National Executive Committee of the NRM 'a forum of ignorant people' when that body is considered to be an important organ of the government, which initiates policies and proposals to be adopted by the National Conference. It was the President himself who introduced the subject of the removal of the presidential term limits to this same forum. This subject was discussed, a resolution was passed and later endorsed by the National Conference. But because I opposed the President's bid, I was now being accused of speaking at the wrong forum. This was the real Museveni – when you did not agree with him, you were accused of speaking at a wrong forum. It didn't matter whether what you said was correct or not; what mattered, apparently, was the forum. Even when Dr Besigye wrote that dossier pointing out all the weaknesses of the Movement government in 2001, the issue became the wrong forum rather than the substance of what he was writing about.

So this time I told the President that I could not understand these contradictions. I said, "Sir, how come that when you, the President, introduced the important issue to such 'ignorant people' it was a right forum for you and all those who supported you, but when I opposed you, it became a wrong forum?" I asked him how he could call those people ignorant and of too low a level for me to address such an important issue when he is the one who introduced it to them. In any case, wasn't the NEC a very high-level organ of the National Resistance Movement?

He replied that as a minister, I should have discussed the issue in cabinet and not at Kyankwanzi. I reminded him that I was at Kyankwanzi not as a minister, but as a member of the NEC representing the women of Mbarara, Bushenyi and Ntungamo and I was expressing the views of those women. Incidentally, the women who had elected me to the NEC, Bernadette Bigirwa (RIP) and Hon Winnie Byanyima also did not support the removal of the term limits. I went on to tell him that, as a minister, I had not had an opportunity to discuss the issue because the day when it was on the agenda for discussion in cabinet, we received instructions that we were not to discuss it before the NEC had met.

President Museveni is so crafty and really excels at scheming. I am sure that his intelligence reports had informed him that the cabinet was not in support of his scheme, and so he knew that if the cabinet had discussed it and rejected it then he would have lost the bid. And so he stopped the cabinet from discussing it and, instead, took it to NEC, which is superior to the cabinet. Once the NEC passed it, the cabinet had no alternative but to endorse it. So taking it to NEC was to preempt rejection by the cabinet. And yet here he was, telling me I should have talked in cabinet and not at the NEC. When I insisted that I was right to have expressed my views at the NEC, he said that even then, I should have talked through Hon Kategaya. But how could I have talked through Hon Kategaya, who incidentally never said anything at Kyankwanzi? Don't I have a mouth of my own? And why talk through somebody else, when everybody else who supported his scheme spoke for themselves? Since when did Matembe ever need to borrow someone else's mouth to talk?

I told him that because NEC, as the National Executive

Committee, was superior to cabinet, there was no way I could have kept quiet and let the NEC make such a crucial decision which I disagreed with, without expressing my views on it.

I added that, "Sir if you think my well-intentioned intervention at the NEC meeting was a terrible thing, then I think I am lost."

"No, you cannot be lost because I will find you," he replied. At this point, he picked a marker and a flip chart and, in his usual condescending and imposing style, started lecturing me about good methods of work. After his winding lecture which revealed nothing new except what he always told us at such meetings to divert us away from the main issues, he said, "I am sure now I have found you."

I replied, "No sir, as a matter of fact, I am lost further." I remember telling him that if this is the way he perceived things, he and I could not get along anymore.

When this exchange between the two of us had gone on for about 40 minutes, in a meeting with about 13 members, Hon Elly Tumwine intervened and brought it to an end. He said that since there were many items on the agenda and the subject we were discussing prematurely was not number one on the agenda, why couldn't we be orderly and start the discussion with the first item? The president agreed and the meeting was re-directed to the first item on the agenda.

Since the items were many and it got late, we never went back to my agenda item. In fact, the meeting ended after we discussed a few things here and there without concretizing anything. When I left that meeting, I knew that my time in office as the Minister for Ethics and Integrity had ended.

I could have resigned but I did not. I did not resign there and then because this matter had not been tabled before cabinet for debate. I decided that once the matter was brought to the cabinet and was passed, I would resign. In fact, three of us, Hon Eriya Kategaya (RIP), the then 1st Deputy Prime Minister and Minister for Internal Affairs, and Hon Sarah Kiyingi Kyama, Minister of State for Internal Affairs and I had earlier agreed to oppose the proposal once it was introduced to cabinet, and if we were defeated, we would resign.

Secondly, since I had already expressed my view on the subject openly in public, I thought it would still serve my purpose if he removed me from his cabinet because it would be known then that he had removed me for opposing his bid for life presidency.

Acting very quickly, probably to avoid embarrassment in case other cabinet members joined us in opposing him, and at the same time to intimidate and silence the other cabinet ministers, Museveni reshuffled his cabinet about three weeks after our Rwakitura meeting. On 23rd May 2013, he dropped me and four other ministers, three of whom opposed his bid for life presidency: Hon Kategaya, Hon Bidandi Ssali, and Hon Sarah Kiyingi Kyama. The fourth minister dropped was Hon Mukasa Muruli. It was after our removal from the cabinet that the issue of removal of term limits was tabled before cabinet, which endorsed it.

After the President had boldly sacked his long-standing childhood friend, Hon Kategaya, and his well-known strong confidante, Miria Matembe, both from his own region Ankole, what would be the fate of any other minister who dared to oppose his bid? His action of reshuffling us out of cabinet for no other reason except for opposing the life presidency bid made it very clear that he was completely determined to get his way come rain or sunshine.

From that day forward, political events in Uganda were never the same. The debate on the removal of the term limits became a hot topic in public fora, on the streets and in the media. The President was an active party in this debate but resorted to abusing us in public meetings and rallies. He even used State House operatives to call us the 'malwa group'. My, it was hot!

The President, who had always despised the peasantry status, started glorifying peasants because he realized that the way the debate was unfolding, the elite class did not support him and his hope lay in the peasants who could be manipulated and exploited to support his bid. So he started playing the peasants against the elite, thinking he could still change the Constitution if it was only the minority elite who opposed him.

Later on, the president learnt that, according to the Constitution, it was Parliament that had the power to amend the provision on the term limits. That is when he devised a strategy to bribe the members of parliament, a strategy that worked well for him.

## Pictorial

Hon Matembe hands over the the office of Minister of Ethics to her successor, Hon Tim Lwanga

Former Mbarara LC5 Chairman, 'Governor' Fred Kamugira receives Hon Matembe at the district headquarters

Hon Matembe embraces former Archbishop of the Church of Uganda, Luke Orombi

Hon Matembe stresses a point to the former Germany Ambassador to Uganda, Klauss Holden while officiating Women's day in Mbarara district

Hon Matembe swears in as Minister of Ethics and Integrity in 2001 in Kampala

Hon Matembe and her Namasagali College old girl, Rt Hon Rebecca Kadaga having a chat with their former headmaster, Fr Grimes

Hon Matembe shares a hearty moment with former Vice President, Dr Specioza Kazibwe

Hon Matembe and Hon Sarah Kiyingi Kyama, then Minister of State for Internal Affairs, peruse the Ssebutinde Commission report

Hon Matembe addressing a symposium on corruption in Gulu town

Hon. Matembe and then police spokeman Asuman Mugenyi addressing Police officers about ethics and integrity

Hon Matembe inspects a guard of honour mounted by Uganda Police at a state function

Hon Matembe being congratulated by the president upon swearing in as a minister in 1998

Hon Matembe shares a word with Charity Ngilu, Kenyan Minister of Health at that time at a conference in Nairobi

Hon Matembe addresses participants of a cadre course about the fight against corruption

Hon Matembe with her former Headmistress, Ms Joan Hall at a Bweranyangi Old Girls event in Kampala.

Justice Kanyeihamba launches Hon Matembe's first book in 2002 in Kampala

Hon Matembe with Eriya Kategaya at an event

Hon Matembe stresses a point to Hon Daudi Migereko. Looking on is Hon Hussein Kyanjo

Hon Matembe with former Kenyan UN representative Deborah Asio and a colleague after conducting a training and mentorship programme of women politicians in Kenya

Hon Matembe walks out of her former office after handing over to Hon Tim Lwanga

Hon Ruth Nankabirwa and Hon Matembe take to the floor for a traditional dance. Looking on is Hon James Kakooza

For her lifelong commitment to the struggle for women empowerment, equality, fairness and justice for all, Victoria University, Canada awarded an honorary Doctorate of Law to Hon Matembe

Mr & Mrs Matembe & children cutting cake at their 25th wedding anniversary

Hon Matembe and her husband opening a dance at their 25th weddding anniversary party

Miria with her husband Nekemia Matembe at their home in Kampala

Miria Matembe with her family. From left are her sons: Grace, Gilbert, Gideon, Godwin; daughters-in-love and grand children

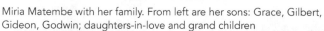

Godwin & Tyna

Bruce & Maud

Grace & Naome

Gilbert & Rachael

## Hon Matembe's children & their Spouses

# Chapter Eight

# Fighting the Lifting of the Presidential Term Limits in Parliament

## Going Back to the Backbench

Following the cabinet reshuffle, when I went back to the backbench in Parliament, I was warmly welcomed by colleagues. They were extremely happy to receive me because they thought that being in the cabinet had constrained me from using my full potential as an effective parliamentarian. My colleagues reinvigorated my drive and resolve when they told me that though I had 'deserted' them, they were glad that I was back to reinforce their work, which was, among other things, to fight the lifting of the presidential term limits.

Before I joined cabinet, I had been an effective debater – questioning and critiquing government policy – but as a cabinet minister, since I was preoccupied with implementing government policies, I spent more time and effort defending them rather than critiquing them. Because many people do not understand how these separate institutions (that is, the Legislature and the Executive) work, some people had been saying that Matembe was in cabinet "busy eating and that's why she was not talking much" in parliament. However, when you are a cabinet minister, you make your criticisms in a different forum which is closed to the public.

Also, as a member of cabinet, you are bound by the principle of collective responsibility, such that when a decision has been taken by the government, you cannot come out to openly oppose it or question it in public, irrespective of your personal opinion of it. The truth is that I had not kept quiet; I was of course speaking out as usual, but in cabinet meetings, and indeed, I often got into trouble for some of the opinions I expressed in cabinet.

In my previous time as a backbencher, before I became a minister, I had been a member of the Legal and Parliamentary Affairs Committee as well as the Rules, Discipline and Privileges Committee. I was re-appointed on these two committees. It was in the Rules, Discipline and Privileges Committee that I was again confronted with the issue of amending the constitution to remove the presidential term limits.

Originally, according to the rules, voting on the removal of the term limits was supposed to be by secret ballot. However, the government quickly moved to seek an amendment of the rules of procedure so as to make voting on this issue open, whereby each individual member would be required to verbally and openly declare YES or NO to the lifting of the term limits. My suspicion was that this change of procedure was sought so that members who had been bribed to support the constitutional amendment would be intimidated and publicly vote in favour of the motion. As a member on that Rules Committee, I vehemently opposed the amendment of this rule of procedure.

## My Spirited Fight Against Life Presidency

The motion to change the procedural rules was forwarded to the Rules, Discipline and Privileges Committee. Hon Ben Wacha was the chairperson of the committee and although I knew he did not agree with the motion, he played neutral and chaired the meeting, even when he knew that the side in favour of amending the rules was bound to win.

I strongly opposed the amendment of the rules whose motive was clearly to hand President Museveni his wish of a life presidency. I also wrote a minority report which was presented to Parliament, in which I tried, to the best of my knowledge and abilities, to justify why the constitution should not be amended. It is on record that in my minority report, I disassociated myself with the entire evil scheme of lifting the presidential term limits because I knew it would expose the country to many problems in future. As events are unfolding in Uganda now, more than fifteen years down the road, and now with the removal of presidential age limit amidst public outcry to retain it, one can see that my fears were very well founded. Unfortunately, because I was in the minority, I still lost out despite my spirited fight in defence of democratic governance and constitutionalism.

Eventually, the constitution was amended and the presidential term limits were removed. What a heart-breaking moment for me!

On Tuesday, July 12th, 2005, by a 220 to 53 vote, with two abstentions, Parliament gave a final approval to the constitutional amendment that scrapped a 2-term limit for presidency. It was one of the saddest moments in my life; I went out of the parliament building and wept like a little child. I cried for my country because I knew that the removal of the term limits was taking this country back to the oppression it had come out of. Once again, my hopes of a better, progressive and non-violent Uganda were shattered.

As far as I was concerned, our internationally acclaimed constitution had been murdered just for the sake of keeping President Museveni in power. I have a personal attachment to the 1995 Constitution because, as noted earlier, I participated in its making, both as commissioner and as a Constituent Assembly (CA) delegate.

Owing to the fact that the 1995 Constitution was made through a popular and participatory process, the issue of the presidential term limits had originated from the citizens themselves. During the educational phase of the exercise, we learnt that people were very concerned about the governance of the country and specifically about presidents who did not want to leave power peacefully. They proposed the limiting of the presidential term to two terms of five years each as a safety net to guard against leaders who clung onto power. They hoped this would guarantee a peaceful transfer of power from one president to another. They were very sure and clear in their minds that unless there was presidential term limits, there was no way a powerful president who controlled the army and the finances would leave power through elections; it had not happened in Uganda. People said that they were tired of wars caused by presidents who never wanted to relinquish power peacefully.

As a commission, we put the people's proposals in the draft constitution. During the debate of the draft, this proposal sailed through smoothly because all of us could see that against our history since independence in 1962, this was the most sensible provision to help us get on the democratic path. This constitution took us five-and-ahalf years to make - four years for the commission to prepare the draft and one-and-half years for the Constituent Assembly to debate and promulgate it. So much time and resources were spent on the constitution-making exercise. In fact, I for one, was able to complete my house using the allowances I received while on this project. And yet here we were destroying what had cost us so much to build simply because of the personal ambitions and greed of one individual. How terribly sad!

I could not believe that Ugandans could allow this to happen, but they did because of corruption. This is why I believe that without decisively dealing with corruption, there is no way we can transform this nation. Imagine, with a mere five million shillings given to each of the members of parliament, save for those who opposed the motion, and our National Constitution was amended to our peril. We are now total slaves to this evil action by our leaders. We are like the brothers of Joseph in the Bible, who sold themselves into slavery by selling their brother out of envy.

I had no doubt in my mind that the removal of the presidential term limits would take Uganda back to the era of conflict and violence due to lack of democratic governance. In fact, Ugandans can be compared to the biblical children of Israel who were released from slavery and set out on a journey of freedom to the Promised Land. However, it took them forty years, on a journey that should have taken eleven days, to cross to the Promised Land. For forty years they were in the desert moving around the mountain, all because of their poor attitude and slave mentality. Likewise, Uganda attained independence over 50 years ago and set out on the road to freedom. Unfortunately, we are still moving in circles in a sea of poverty, ignorance, disease greed and corruption, with almost no hope of ever crossing to the Promised Land.

At the time President Museveni was campaigning for the removal of the term limits, his team coined a slogan 'kisanja' meaning 'third term'. Thus, the project of removing the term limits was being addressed in a deceitful manner. While the public thought that they were giving a mere third (and last) term to President Museveni, the amendment was to remove the term limits altogether, paving way for his life presidency. Some of us were wiser and knew better. During the debates in Parliament and public fora such as radio talk shows, I kept reminding the public that this was not just about a third term. Indeed, some people correctly labeled it a 'sad term' because surely it evoked sadness. Hadn't the President shamelessly lied, on **Page 9 of his 2001 Presidential Manifesto**, that it would be his last term before retiring? For me, I knew the President was removing the term limits because he wanted to rule forever.

I have since learnt that one of the things that strongly motivated President Museveni's life presidency project was the discovery of oil, or 'my oil' as he calls it. Apparently, he believes that the oil is his personal possession. Can you imagine? The man was not prepared to go without enjoying the oil money. He used to say it in cabinet: "Now we are getting okay; we shall be alright. These donors, they will keep quiet."

Once you remove the presidential term limits in Africa, and especially in Uganda, all you need to do to remain in power is to "buy" people or intimidate them; you hold violent elections and you rig and so on. Unfortunately, my fear has come to pass and I see no end to it. As we all know, here in Africa where the majority of the people are rural-based, poor, uneducated and uninformed, it is extremely difficult to remove a head of state through the electoral process. This is why many countries on the continent have opted for presidential term limits, and it has worked to bring about peaceful transfers of power from one president to another where it has been applied, such as in neighbouring Kenya and Tanzania. Since President Museveni took power in 1986, Tanzania has had four presidents, while Kenya has had three. We are now trapped with a president who has no intention of ever leaving power, even after more than thirty years. I believe even those who were at the forefront of the bid to remove the term limits, like Hon Amama Mbabazi and Hon Hope Mwesigye, have since lived to deeply regret their actions.

## Collegues to Foes: Is Political Opposition Enemity?

Between the time of the Kyankwanzi Resolution and the amendment of the Constitution to remove the presidential term limits, there was a fierce battle of words that was played out in the public arena between the President and his erstwhile allies now turned 'enemies' because of their opposition to the removal of the term limits. The most vocal opponents of the *kisanja* project included Hon Eriya Kategaya, Hon Prof George Kanyeihamba, Hon Bidandi Ssali and myself.

In characteristic Museveni style, he went into panic mode and moved from rally to rally, from one talk show to another in an effort to negate the dissenting voices. He said that our contributions in the Movement struggle did not matter and as such, he was calling upon Ugandans to shun our message. He attempted to rewrite history by labelling us useless people whose opinion should not matter. In a matter of days, President Museveni turned from friend to foe of anyone who dared to disagree with him.

When the President went to Mbarara District, some people, especially the women I represented, expressed their displeasure with him for dropping me from the cabinet, just because I opposed the *kisanja*. He went primitive and really abused us and called us all sorts of names. He called Hon Kazoora and I *omweziga* – millet husks. He said, "You see this Matembe is like millet husks; the left-overs you discard after pounding millet." Inadvertently, President Museveni was telling the country that he was an opportunistic and selfish leader, since to him, you are useful only when you are on his side.

In another instance, he said Hon Bidandi Ssali's leaving the NRM was inconsequential because he was 'a mere peg in the wheel'. Imagine such lack of basic decorum to a comrade who had stood by him all along and worked to help grow the Movement since the days of the Uganda Patriotic Movement (UPM) back in the 1980s!

On another occasion, the President said that Justice Kanyeihamba was only fit to judge simple cases of chicken theft and the like. Imagine Prof Kanyeihamba, a distinguished constitutional and human rights lawyer and author of several books, was being declared incompetent and unsuited to comment on constitutional issues and only fit for simple cases, simply because he was opposed to the constitutional amendment!

In another of his media outbursts, the President called his comrade and long-time colleague, Hon Eriya Kategaya, a traitor, and said Hon Ruzindana was good for nothing. Like a wounded buffalo, Museveni was so angry and incensed that he denied their critical roles in the NRA liberation struggle.

## President Museveni Attempts to Woo Us Back into His Government

After being subjected to such abuse, humiliation and dehumanization, I was extremely surprised when, after the removal of the constitutional term limits, the President tried to woo some of us back into his government. He actually invited Hon Eriya Kategaya, Hon Richard Kaijuka, Hon Amanya Mushega and myself to meet with him three times and tried to convince us to rejoin his NRM party, claiming that he needed us to be with him if his party was to be strong. I did not attend the third meeting because I was out of the country so I do not know what transpired, but not long after that, Hon Eriya Kategaya rejoined his government.

In the first meeting, President Museveni acknowledged that our point of departure was the amendment of the constitution to remove the presidential term limits. He added that since the problem between us had been solved by the removal of the provision of the term limits, there was now nothing to disagree about and therefore we should get together again and work with him. This was very annoying to me. The manner in which the President presented the matter to us led me to believe that he didn't understand what it meant to be a principled person. He apparently could not distinguish between disagreement on an issue and disagreement on a principle. The simplistic way in which he talked about the fundamental issue of removing the term limits was to me very strange and devious. Simply because he had achieved his ambition he thought he could ignore our shattered hopes. By the way, he had held a huge feast at State House to celebrate the death of our safety net. Did he think this was something we could easily overcome and quickly jump onto his bandwagon to mess up our nation along with him? Not at all!

## "I Am the Only Man with a Vision"

In the first meeting, President Museveni had many things to say, as he once again laboured to justify the removal of the presidential term limits. He started with his customary chest-thumping talk of him being the only visionary Ugandan leader. Before us, he said without shame: "Look here, there is nobody else who can lead this nation; there is no one with a vision to move Uganda forward."

Secondly, he recycled the excuse of the East African integration. On this matter, he said that if he died before the integration of East Africa, he would not rest in his grave. He went on to tell us all his usual stuff about African integration and how as a Pan-Africanist he was still very much needed by Africa for its development. Generally, he didn't tell us anything new, but the usual talk about his vision and indispensability.

I informed him that the integration of East Africa was a principle that could be carried on by any other leader who assumed the mantle after him. Therefore there was no need for him to illegitimately and deceitfully use such empty talk to hold Ugandans at ransom. Therefore, there was no need for fear that the integration would fail after his departure. I also expressed my view that there are many Ugandans who have a vision for the country but only need the opportunity and space to execute their vision.

I saw this as an opportunity to let him know all my thoughts and opinions on these matters. One thing I am very happy about is that, although I parted company with President Museveni, I had an opportunity to say all I wanted to say about what I thought of him. Whatever I had left unsaid at the Kyankwanzi meeting, I was able to let out in those two meetings. He also knows that I was and still remain sincere about whatever I said and still say for it is in the interest of the nation and moreover for his own good too.

During the first meeting, I told him I was very scared that he was going to either put me in prison or kill me. I explained that when I spoke my mind at Kyankwanzi, he dropped me from the cabinet. Now that I was going to say more, what would he do if he got annoyed, wouldn't he order for my imprisonment or for my killing?

The President wondered why I would think so, as if he had ever killed anybody. I reminded him that he had killed people during the war in Luweero. He responded by saying that they were at war then and he was killing enemies. I told him that was the reason why I was scared, because now that I disagreed with him, I was an enemy and could be killed. He was very surprised that I was thinking that way about him.

In his own words, the president swore to me that he would never put me in prison or kill me. He said, *"Mbwenu Matembe, buzima notiina ngu ninza kukwita? Mbwenu hati nakurahirira tihariho obundiba nkukomire nari nkwitsire,"* loosely translated as: Matembe, I give you my word. Under my watch, you will never be arrested or killed.

At the second meeting, I told him that to me, he, Obote and Amin were the same in as far as abrogating the National Constitution was concerned. He abrogated it through corruption by bribing members of parliament to amend it. Obote, by making a 'pigeon hole' one, and Amin, by simply abolishing it.

I added that I no longer believed in him since I discovered that I had followed a person I did not know, in fact, an impostor. I was very candid. I told him I had followed one person but they were now two in one. Demonstrating with my hand, I told him I joined one who looked like the face of my hand, but now the one I saw was like the back of my hand. So I asked him, "Which one of you is calling me to re-join him? I joined you when you were travelling along a certain clear path, but now you have abandoned that path and have jumped into the bush without a clear direction, how can I join you?" I could no longer rejoin him because he was not the person I had joined in the first place. I told him I simply could not join him again because, as they say, once bitten, twice shy. I told him that he had betrayed me so much and shattered my hopes for the country. He asked me who I was going to join and I said I was going with nobody except Jesus.

I remember quoting for him Lord Acton's famous saying: "Power corrupts; absolute power corrupts absolutely." To that he responded, "Oh, Matembe, you think it's power that is making me do what I am doing?"

I said, "Yes it is, what else do you think it is?"

He replied, "It is struggle. I struggle for the African people and I will continue to struggle until they are free."

I reminded him that he was not the only person struggling, that I too was struggling for gender equality and women's empowerment and that he was spoiling the environment for my struggle. To that, he responded that since we were both 'strugglists', he was inviting me to join him again so that we can continue with our struggles. That's when I laughed and told him he was not serious and I said goodbye to him.

It is important to note that previously while the lifting of the presidential term limits debate was raging internationally, David White, a *Financial Times* journalist had asked Museveni if he was going to stand for the third term. His answer, less cryptic this time than the vague "I will follow the constitution" was rather telling. He answered that the question was "irrelevant, as long as there is agreement on the way forward, what does it matter who is in charge? Africa hasn't been lacking a turnover of leaders, what has been lacking has been **vision**".

## Clamping Down on Political Parties

On this occasion, I also told him that it was unfortunate that he had lost the chance to create a legacy by peacefully handing over power to another president. But I reminded him that there was another opportunity that he could embrace, which was to let the other political parties form and organize themselves to compete for power peacefully. I reminded him that all along, we had thought that the National Resistance Movement was going to mother and nurture good political parties. As it had turned out, two political parties had been born out of the Movement, namely the Forum for Democratic Change (FDC) and the National Resistance Movement party (NRM).

I asked him to let FDC, and its then leader Colonel Dr Kizza Besigye, organize and mobilise members to build a strong opposition without disturbance and harassment. That would enable healthy competition among the political parties in the next general elections. I told him that since he had been in the field for so long, he would be able to win. But ultimately, he could salvage some pride and honor for himself and create a legacy by allowing the country to peacefully transform into a good multiparty democracy.

At that meeting, the President promised that he was

going to let political parties organize themselves and mobilise members without his interference. So when Dr Besigye was immediately arrested and prosecuted on trumped up charges, the little grain of trust left in me for Museveni disappeared completely.

Having removed the presidential term limits from the constitution, at least Museveni should have created a conducive environment for the political parties to organize themselves without harassment. But this has not been the case. Lifting the ban on political parties was not of much use since the parties continue to be suffocated, demonised and harassed. How can there be democracy without a strong opposition to keep the government in check? To Museveni, political opposition means enmity; up to now he calls opposition members terrorists, bandits, wolves and enemies.

The crux of the matter is that President Museveni has never wanted multiparty democracy. He had always said that if the country decided to go back to multiparty politics, he would retreat to his home in Rwakitura and watch as the country crumbled and people hacked each other with machetes. Therefore, it is clear that he had reluctantly agreed to open up the political space; because he wanted to stay in power, he had no alternative but to legitimise his stay by opening up the political space.

Since the ban on political parties was lifted in 2005, the opposition parties have not had a conducive environment in which to operate. They can rarely hold peaceful meetings without harassment, intimidation, beating, attacks from the police with teargas and so on. So how can they build themselves into strong institutions capable of competing for power?

Worse still, in his first public statement after his widely disputed victory in the 2016 elections, President Museveni declared that he was going to wipe out all opposition parties and members by 2021. Indeed, he started by appointing key opposition figures into his cabinet and bribing others with presidential appointments. But perhaps, his most lethal method so far has been military brutalization, torture and harassment like was meted out the opposition MPs during Age limit debate and to Hon Robert Kyagulanyi and colleagues during the Arua municipality bye-elections in 2018.

# Chapter Nine

## Museveni's Government and the Gender Question – Not Yet Uhuru

### The False Dawn of Women Empowerment

We cannot run away from the truth that Museveni's National Resistance Movement redeemed Uganda from a hopeless situation. By the time Museveni took over government, we had become desperate and many of us had lost hope. So to me, it was like being resurrected from the dead.

I embraced the Movement with such enthusiasm, energy and total commitment because I trusted it and had confidence that it was committed to the principle of gender equality and women's empowerment.

Never before in the history of Uganda had there been such a conducive political environment and goodwill for the participation of women in politics and governance. It reminded me of the Kiganda proverb, *Kyembadde njagaliza embazi Kibuyaga assude,*which means that the wind has felled what I had all along wanted to cut down with an axe.

I was able to utilise this conducive political environment to mobilise the public and espouse the cause for gender equality and women's empowerment. My appointment to the Uganda Constitutional Commission in 1989, which coincided with my election as the Chairperson of Action for Development (ACFODE)- a non-governmental organisation set up to work for women's rights and empowerment in the same year, strengthened my position as a parliamentarian and gave me a national platform through which to espouse the cause.

My work as a commissioner enabled me to traverse Uganda and mobilise both men and women to contribute to the constitution-making process so as to make a national constitution that would, among other things, promote and protect women's rights. This was indeed done, as evidenced by the National Constitution that was promulgated in 1995 - which contained comprehensive provisions for the promotion and protection of women's rights.

I left no stone unturned in my efforts to promote gender equality and women's empowerment. I was genuinely enthused because I totally believed that Museveni's government was genuinely committed to the cause.

However, after the promulgation of the new constitution, it proved extremely difficult to secure laws for the protection of women's rights. It became an uphill task to implement the constitution as far as the enactment of gender laws was concerned. Beginning with the failure to secure land co-ownership rights for women within two years of the implementation of the constitution, to the inability to pass the law on marriage and divorce after over 20 years since the bill was first tabled before Parliament, we met a lot of challenges.

During the parliamentary and cabinet debates for the enactment of the land law, my eyes were opened to the disturbing fact that the government was not as genuinely committed to the cause as we had been made to believe. We failed to gain the inclusion of the land co-ownership clause in the new land law partly because President Museveni was totally against it. It was then that I woke up to the shocking realisation that Museveni's government was in no way totally or genuinely committed to the equality and empowerment of women.

It was very agonising for me to try and convince the cabinet, and especially President Museveni, on the need and importance of women to co-own with their spouses just that piece of land they use for their sustenance; the land from which they get their livelihood as subsistence farmers. The President was opposed to the issue, saying that women were greedy and would want to rob their husbands of their land. I explained to him that in fact the clause was about co-ownership between spouses, meaning that even when the land belonged to the wife, the husband would also have the right of co-ownership.

Strangely enough, on hearing this, some senior women ministers rose up in arms against me asserting that there was no way they would accept a clause that would allow their spouses to co-own their land. I was shocked to see these women join the President in opposing the co-ownership of land for women because of their own selfish interests. Simply because they were land owners, they looked at the clause from the perspective of their own personal interests. I remember vividly the words of Hon Dr Specioza Wandira Kazibwe, who was the Vice President then; Hon Sydah Bumba, by then the Minister for Energy; and also Hon Namirembe Bitamazire, then Minister for Education and, moreover, the Chairperson of the National Association of Women's Non governmental Organisation (NAOWO), as they joined the President in opposing me on the co-ownership clause in the cabinet meetings.

After listening to their statements against co-owning their land with their spouses, President Museveni said, "Matembe, do you hear your fellow women? Why don't you behave like them?"

I told him, "Mr President, sir, I am a different brand of a woman."

I remember Hon Mukiibi Benigna, and some men including Hon Baguma Isoke and Hon Mondo Kagonyera spoke passionately in support of the clause. Unfortunately, the rest of the cabinet members looked on as I tussled it out with the President. Finally, the discussion was brought to its futile conclusion when the women 'of substance' threw their weight behind the President to kill the clause completely and decisively.

Since my fellow women had opposed me, I of course lost out on the second bid to revive the co-ownership clause by way of amendment to the land law. The details about this issue are recorded in my autobiography published in 2002. That was the beginning of my loss of trust and confidence in Museveni's commitment to the women's cause.

In Uganda, land is the main resource people have; without it one is poor and powerless. Culturally, women do not own or control land. Only those rich enough to buy it and those few allowed to inherit it from their parents own land. These are extremely few. So the co-ownership clause was meant to give married women some economic security by giving them the right to co-own land with their spouses. In its coverage, the clause referred only to that piece of land that comprised the matrimonial home and the surrounding area used for the sustainance of the family. The clause did not extend co-ownership to the big chunks of land and/or big farms that may be owned by the husband or the wife. So why was it extremely difficult for the President to accept this small token for women? Perhaps because it would give the majority of women some security and power and therefore protect them to some degree from future manipulation by his government.

It was then that I remembered and regretted why I had not listened to my big sister, Hon Cecilia Ogwal, when we were enacting the Women and Youth Councils statutes.

She was strongly opposed to the enactment of these two laws, arguing that they would be tools for recruiting women and youth, as was done in communist countries, to use them to serve the government's interests rather than their own interests. While I saw the Women and Youth Councils statutes as instruments for empowerment and political participation, my sister Hon Cecilia Ogwal saw them as tools of patronage to hold women and youth captive as they served the government's interests rather than their own. Indeed, that is what is happening now. I wish I had known!

Just like in Dr Besigye's case which I have already detailed, where I did not believe him when he claimed that Museveni would never leave power willingly, I was once again proved wrong by Hon Cecilia Ogwal. I came to realize that indeed both the women and youth in Uganda have been co-opted into state structures and thus have been disempowered by government through manipulation, exploitation, bribery and intimidation to work against their own interests. Due to massive corruption, intimidation and poverty, politically active women and youth in Uganda are unable to disentangle themselves from the clutch of the state and they have become instruments against their own cause.

Museveni's version of empowerment of women means women dancing and singing the rhetoric of 'our man' "No change" and the sheer opportunity to participate without any real influence on the governance agenda. When it comes to the empowerment of women through effective policies, laws and programs, Museveni and his government are not interested. I hope my story will be an eye-opener for the 'yellow girls'(women in the Movement party) to see the predicament of women in Uganda.

As a matter of fact, it is not women alone that Museveni does not want empowered. In my opinion, President Museveni fears and resents any empowered person. He prefers to keep people ignorant, poor and divided so that he can manipulate, exploit and easily rule them. Unfortunately, it took me a long time to realize this and so I lent him a hand in mobilizing women to his side under a false illusion that he indeed was committed to our cause.

## The Quota System/Affirmative Action

When the principle of affirmative action was constitutionalised and women councils were formed for organising women within the political system, I thought that the women of Uganda were going to be empowered to influence the governance agenda and make it responsive to their needs, interests and concerns. The quota system, commonly known as affirmative action in Uganda, has been the most successful strategy used to increase women's political participation the world over. However, whether their participation is effective depends on the nature of the quota system; how it is designed and implemented. The quota system can be a double-edged sword.

On the one hand it has obliged men to include women in decision-making processes since public spaces must create room for women. Since it is the men who open up these spaces because they are in them already, they tend to seek out women who they will be able to manipulate; women who will readily accept men's hegemony. For example, many governments have been able to demonstrate that they are in favour of promoting women's participation while at the same time making sure that these seats are taken by token women who can be controlled. This leads to a scenario where you have women in positions of power but without real power. The only power such females have is the power to serve powerful males; a situation that is worse, in some cases, than not being in power at all.

Uganda has been applying the quota system commonly known as affirmative action for over 33 years now. It was introduced on the political scene with the advent of the National Resistance Movement government in 1986. This system was later constitutionalised in the 1995 National Constitution and has since then been implemented in Parliament and local government councils through the Parliamentary Elections Act and the Local Government Act.

The constitution says:

> *32.   (1)  Notwithstanding   anything   in   this Constitution, the State shall take affirmative action in favour of groups marginalized on the basis of gender, age, disability or any other reason created by history, tradition or custom, for the purpose of redressing imbalances which exist against them. 33. (5) Without prejudice to article 32 of this Constitution,   women   shall   have   the   right   to*

*affirmative action for the purpose of redressing the imbalances created by history, tradition or custom.*

Coupled with the principle of gender balance that is also enshrined in the Constitution, the principle of affirmative action has enabled women to increasingly participate in politics and governance.

The Directive Principle of State Policy V says thus:

*"The state shall ensure gender balance and fair representation of all marginalized groups on all constitutional and other bodies.*

As already mentioned, the National Constitution provides for the reservation of special seats for women in parliament through the creation of a specific geographical constituency known as a district to be competed for by women only. Originally these constituencies were very large, covering an average of 4 to 8 ordinary constituencies, and the election of women was through electoral colleges. At present, so many districts have been carved out of the large ones. Though some of them are still bigger than ordinary constituencies, many of them are now equal in size to the ordinary constituencies. At the same time, women are entitled to contest in the other ordinary constituencies (open seats) with their male counterparts. Elections are by universal suffrage.

Further, the National Constitution and the Local Government Act provide for not less than a third of all the seats in the local government councils to be reserved for women. The Constitution also specifically provides for the periodic review of affirmative action with the aim of assessing its continued relevance.

Incidentally, the Constitution of Uganda is one of the most gender-sensitive constitutions in the world. In addition to providing for the quota system, it dedicates a whole article of six comprehensive clauses for the promotion and protection of women's rights. Therefore, on the face of it, the women of Uganda appear to be doing quite well. Beneath the surface however, this is yet to be confirmed.

## Achievements

As noted by Elizabeth Kharono in her report *Review of Affirmative Action in Uganda (July 2003)*, despite the many challenges associated with affirmative action, it has registered a number of achievements in promoting women's participation in politics and governance. It is the single means of entry into politics and governance that has resulted in the most significant female participation in public decision-making.

If one considers the number of women parliamentarians who have continuously been voted in through the open seats, it is clear that if there was no affirmative action, only about 8% of the members of parliament would be women.

Representation of women in local government structures has also been significantly increased as a result of affirmative action. This is particularly important for the improvement of the status of women because it is at the local council levels (LCV and LCIII) where planning, budgeting and prioritisation of needs and concerns of the people are done.

The increased number of women in politics and governance has enhanced their visibility in public life, legitimised their presence in areas previously considered to be male domains, as well as demystifying public offices such as those of the vice president, minister for finance and minister for defence. Previously, if a woman was ever appointed a minister, it would be for education, women's affairs or at best, health. But in Uganda, we have broken through that gender barrier. Women have now held major portfolios such as Vice President, Minister for Finance, Minister for Agriculture, Speaker of Parliament, Deputy Chief Justice, Minister for Energy and Minister for Defence. Women no longer think that certain positions belong to men only. They are so inspired and motivated by the new possibilities, that we have had three women contest for the presidency: in 2006, 2011 and 2016.

The creation of women role models through affirmative action has motivated many young women in Uganda and has built their confidence; they now see themselves as capable of rising up to such positions. In fact, we have quite a number of young women now in Parliament and in the cabinet. The political environment has also become more favourable to women, such that more women are now willing to stand for elections for both the open seats as well as the reserved seats; this was not the case before affirmative action.

Even though patriarchal attitudes and practices still exist, it is evident that there is increased awareness of gender issues and the importance of women's participation in politics among Ugandans. Affirmative action has contributed to making the political landscape richer and more diverse and has led to a broad acceptance of women as leaders. In fact, in areas where women have been outstanding performers, the electorate is very open to electing women for the open seats. For example, by the time I left politics in 2006, we had three women members of parliament from the greater Mbarara, including myself, whereas in 1989, I was the only female member of parliament out of eleven from the same district.

The increased political participation of women has greatly enhanced their skills and self-confidence as well as built their capacity as legislators and leaders. Women now head major committees of parliament and local government councils, which was not the case before.

## Weaknesses of Affirmative Action

I regret to say that despite all these achievements, women's participation has not had the desired impact on the governance agenda to make it more responsive and sensitive to women's equality and empowerment. Research conducted in 2007 by the Centre for Women in Governance (CEWIGO) in the sectors of health, education and family laws shows that women's political participation has not substantially influenced the formation and implementation of policies, legislations and programs for the betterment of women.

# Why is this?

There are two main reasons:

The first, and biggest, weakness of affirmative action as applied in Uganda is the lack of ownership by its beneficiaries: women and women's organisations. This lack of ownership may have been caused by the way affirmative action came about. The system was introduced using a top-down approach; it was created at the will of the NRM government rather than arising from intense pressure by the women themselves right from the grassroots.

This being the case, women were not able to shape its nature and devise rules governing its implementation. Perhaps if it had come about as a result of women's own demands, the women would have been more involved in shaping it in a way that would benefit them. As it stands now, the quota system in Uganda has been perceived by women as a gift from above that came to them as a favor but not as a right.

This is extremely unfortunate, considering the tremendous effort and unity demonstrated by Ugandan women during the constitution-making process. The gender sensitive National Constitution was not given to us as a gift; it was the result of hard, dedicated and enthusiastic work of the women of Uganda throughout the process; right from the Constitutional Commission itself, up through the Constituent Assembly, to the promulgation of the constitution by the Constituent Assembly. The women of Uganda put up a spirited fight to ensure that the constitution paid adequate attention to women's rights, interest and needs.

I regret to say that the spirit of the constitution has not been fully exploited to translate into adequate laws and policies for the general empowerment of the women of Uganda.

This perception of affirmative action as a 'gift' illustrates the failure of its proponents to own, engage and define its content as well as failure to develop a coherent and strategic agenda for its implementation. Because of these failures, most of the women beneficiaries not only feel indebted to the government, but they also dare not challenge the status quo in case they bite the hand that feeds them. They are more comfortable fitting into the system rather than trying to transform the cultures and structures that marginalise them, the latter being the very reason affirmative action was introduced.

In fact, one can rightly say that affirmative action in Uganda has largely become counterproductive. On the one hand, it is used as a job opportunity for those who take up these positions. This is reflected in the complacency and self-satisfaction that is sometimes exhibited by some female MPs and local government councillors. As argued by Dr Sylvia Tamale in her book, *When Hens Begin to Crow (2000)*, a good number of female politicians who run for office aspire for increased personal benefits – just like many male politicians – and are not motivated by, and do nothing about gender equality and women's empowerment issues.

On the other hand, the government has turned affirmative action into a patronage system for the purpose of co-opting women into state structures. The government is increasingly using affirmative action through the creation of many unviable districts and constituencies to attract more women into parliament and thus hold them psychologically at ransom.

Unfortunately, the quality of women now joining parliament through affirmative action is becoming poorer as these seats no longer attract quality women with a passion for gender equality, but mainly attract those seeking jobs and are loyal to the government.

The situation has been made worse by expensive elections. Elections have become so costly that mainly those women who are loyal to the government and can be sponsored by it are able to win. As a matter of fact, currently the overwhelming majority of the women members of parliament (as well as the men) belong to the ruling NRM, and they spend most of their time lobbying and pushing forward government policies even when these policies are not in the best interest of the women.

A case in point is the rejection of the proposed law on marriage and divorce by the 9th Parliament, which referred to it as a bad law that was aimed at promoting the breakdown of marriages. It was unbelievable to see so many women parliamentarians oppose a law that was intended to empower women, the very constituency whose interests these women leaders were meant to promote and protect.

The fact is, the government lacks the political will to utilise affirmative action as a strategy to promote gender equality and women's empowerment; it is only satisfied with having women occupy the political space without any real influence. As a result, the participation of women in politics and governance has not translated into policies, laws and programs that promote and protect women's rights and interests.

For example, we have had women in the positions of Vice President and ministers for Agriculture, Water, Health and Finance but what have we got as a result? Is there more money in women's pockets? Do we have more water in the homes? Are women benefiting from their agricultural produce? Are women more healthy? And yet when we cry out for women, we are reminded of all the positions women hold in government. We are asked, "What do you want? What don't you have? We have women in top positions, what else do you want? Those of us who express our dissatisfaction with the situation are labelled ungrateful and betrayers of President Museveni.

The second weakness created by affirmative action has been the absence of an implementation framework informed by appropriate policies, laws and institutions. Article 32 of the Constitution anticipated the operationalisation of affirmative action through the passing of requisite laws and the establishment of an institution responsible for their implementation. Apart from the Parliamentary Act and the Local Government Act which provide for affirmative action, no other laws have been passed. It was only in 2007 that the law establishing the Equal Opportunities Commission was passed and the commission constituted.

These legislative shortfalls have hampered the full

implementation of affirmative action, limiting it only to representation in politics, which has overshadowed its other aspects. This has resulted in the thinking that affirmative action is confined to political representation, and yet on its own, political representation cannot redress the gender imbalance and dis-empowerment of women in Uganda if other sectors are not addressed.

Another weakness has been the 'deputy syndrome', signifying tokenism. The trend has been to appoint women in deputy positions thus feminising them. For example, we have previously had a female vice president, female deputy speaker and Deputy Chief Justice but only the Deputy Speaker has since risen to full speakership. In 2006, 32% of the vice chairpersons and 17% of the deputy speakers of local government councils were women. Similarly, on the parliamentary committees, the tendency has been to appoint women as deputies, although a few women are now becoming chairpersons. It brings few real gains for women to be deputies under men because the real power lies with the heads and not the deputies. So it only creates an appearance that women have some authority, when in many cases, deputies never get the opportunity to exercise power. Ironically, women are then perceived as being as powerful as men and even a threat to men, when this is hardly the case.

Incidentally, even affirmative action as it is now applied, in terms of quotas, has not been extended to other bodies such as the cabinet, the executive committees of local government councils, the judiciary, and public service. This is a huge omission because it is in these bodies that major policies and decisions are made, and yet the appointing authority is left with the discretion of appointing anybody he wants. He is only bound by the principle of gender balance, which is usually abused by appointing one or two women, moreover as deputies, as we see for instance with the Human Rights Commission, Electoral Commission and other constitutional bodies.

## What Next? What should be done?

For effective impact, there is a need to go beyond affirmative action, which merely increases the numbers of women in public roles, and address the structural causes of gender imbalance. Placing women in positions of leadership without dismantling the existing patriarchal, social and political structures and systems that had constrained women in the first place, and still do, will not achieve much.

Secondly, the laws establishing quotas to address gender imbalance must be carefully worded to avoid interpretations that may be detrimental to the interest of the intended beneficiaries.

Thirdly, a specific institution responsible for the implementation of the quota system must be established. This institution must be able to spell out the quota system's content, and procedures for implementation, monitoring and evaluation.

Fourthly, the quota system must be demand-driven by the beneficiaries, who must own it, design it and monitor its implementation. Otherwise, left to the will of the leadership that grants it, it may misfire,as it has in our case in Uganda,where women have been taken hostage by the very system that was meant to liberate them.

Fifthly, in order to avoid a situation where beneficiaries feel trapped by the state, or perceive affirmative action as a favour and not a right, women need to maintain a critical distance from the state and establish independent organisations through which they can challenge the inequalities existing within the patriarchal state and critique the government's implementation of affirmative action policies and programs.

One of the biggest challenges faced by Ugandan women now, is how to disentangle themselves from the state 'capture' and patronage. This capture has weakened the women's movement at large because active members in it who operate outside state structures are perceived as enemies of the state when they challenge the status quo of inequality, and yet most women inside the state structures have been 'captured' and are much less capable of challenging the status quo.

The sixth point is that there is a need to develop strategies to ensure that constitutions and manifestos of political parties support women's real and not apparent participation in politics and governance by including effective provisions for affirmative action. These constitutions must also provide for practical ways and means of realising the principle of affirmative action.

# Chapter Ten

# No Political Will to Fight Corruption

## The Inspectorate of Government

Originally established in 1986 by the NRM government, the Inspectorate of Government (IG) was initially referred to as the Office of the Inspector General of Government (OIGG). At that time, it was charged with the general duty of protecting and promoting human rights and the rule of law as well as eliminating and fostering the elimination of corruption and abuse of public offices. The responsibility for the promotion and protection of human rights was later transferred to the Uganda Human Rights Commission (UHRC).

The Inspectorate of Government was initially established by the Inspector General of Government (IGG) statute in 1988. However, with the promulgation of the Uganda Constitution in 1995, the Inspectorate of Government is now entrenched therein under Chapter 13, which prescribes its mandate, functions and powers and other relevant matters. The IG is an independent institution charged with the responsibility of eliminating corruption, and abuse of authority and public office. The powers as enshrined in the Constitution and the IG Act include to; investigate or cause investigation, arrest or cause arrest, prosecute or cause prosecution, make orders and give directions during investigations; access and search – enter and inspect premises or property or search a person or bank account or safe deposit box among others.

### Jurisdiction and Independence of the IG

Article 226 and 227 of the Constitution provides the IG with areas of authority and independence. The jurisdiction of the IG covers officers or leaders whether employed in the public service or not, and also such institutions, organisations or enterprises as Parliament may prescribe by law. The office is independent in the performance of its functions and is only responsible to Parliament.

### Functions of the IG

* *  *To promote and foster strict adherence to the rule of law and principles of natural justice in administration;*

* *To eliminate and foster the elimination of corruption, abuse of authority and public office;*

* *To promote fair, efficient and good governance in public offices; subject to the provision of the Constitution, to supervise the enforcement of the Leadership Code of Conduct;*

* *To enforce the Leadership Code of Conduct;*

* *To investigate any act, omission, advice, decision or recommendation by a public officer or any other authority to which this article applies, taken, made, given or done in exercise for administrative functions; and*

* *To stimulate public awareness about the values of constitutionalism in general and the activities of the office, in particular, through any media and other means it considers appropriate.*

## Battles with the Ministry of Justice

Throughout my life, I have been a vocal and fearless anti-corruption crusader, but it was, perhaps, my appointment as Minister for Ethics and Integrity that brought me into the epicentre of Uganda's "fight against corruption".

Paradoxically, the Ministry of Justice, which is responsible for the administration of justice, and which was supposed to be an ally in fighting corruption, turned its guns towards us at the Ministry of Ethics and Integrity. By the time Hon Janat Mukwaya was appointed the Minister for Justice, the IG was involved in investigating shoddy procurement contracts for the Electoral Commission and some other contracts involving compensation and out-of-court settlements within the Ministry of Justice. For reasons best known to herself, probably in support of her ministry, Hon Janat Mukwaya chose to side with the Electoral Commission and officials from her ministry, especially the then acting Solicitor General, Mr Lucien Tibaruha.

Justice Jotham Tumwesigye was the IGG by then. Hon Janat Mukwaya wrote some offensive letters to the IGG accusing him of interfering with her ministry's work. She sought my co-operation in harassing the IGG. I, of course, refused because as the Minister for Ethics and Integrity, the IGG was my key partner and right hand in the fight against corruption. Therefore, his success and effectiveness was also my success.

I told Hon Janat Mukwaya that the office of the IGG was an institution established by the government to fight corruption in government, and as such, investigating corruption in procurement contracts was not interference with the work of the government but was actually the key mandate of the IGG. Her complaint was that the investigations were derailing the work in her ministry. When she realised that I would not become her accomplice in fighting the IGG, she turned her guns on me. Further, she took the battle to cabinet and started vociferously calling for the trimming of the powers vested in the Inspectorate of Government.

Initially, I had thought that she resented only the institution of the IG, but as time went on, I realised that she resented the holder of the office too. She went as far as labelling us tribalistic, saying that after all Tumwesigye and I were Banyankore and that is why I supported him. But for sure I didn't support the IGG because of his being a Munyankore, which, incidentally, he is not. I supported the institution, irrespective of the person heading it because we were united together in our efforts to fight corruption. Whatever tribe the IGG would have been, be it a Muganda, Langi or any other, I would have supported him or her.

## Attempts to Fight My Ministry and Make it Fail

When Hon Janat Mukwaya took her anti-IGG crusade to cabinet, to my shock, there was a sizable number of ministers who didn't like the IGG and my office. They ganged up against me personally and my ministry.

It was not only Hon Janat Mukwaya and corrupt officials that were baying for my blood and my ministry's failure, but also other cabinet colleagues who were involved in unethical and immoral conduct. As Minister for Ethics and Integrity, any accusation against a minister from the public, whether over corruption or personal conduct related to other ethical values, would be put to me, and as a minister I had to respond. For example, some minister's wives and other women would report to me cases such as adultery, wife-beating, and child and family neglect and I would confront the ministers allegedly involved in such misconduct. Some of the responses and comments I made annoyed my colleagues and they would put me to task, asking who I was to poke my nose into their personal affairs.

My bold approach to these issues did not go down well with them. But being the person that I am, I stuck to my guns and told them that if they wanted, they had better work to remove the ministry, but for as long as it existed and I led it, I would do my work without fear or favour. They had to either behave ethically or quit public office. In my view, as long as public officers behaved unethically, it did not matter whether it was over personal or official matters. I told them once they become public figures, they cease to have personal issues because they have opened up their entire lives to public scrutiny. As it was, some of my cabinet colleagues now looked at me as a pain and saboteur in their 'deals', while others said I was policing their 'personal' matters.

It was no surprise that I had a very rough time presenting both the IGG Statute and the Leadership Code to cabinet for discussion and approval. The resistance from cabinet colleagues was so fierce that it took me almost three years to get those bills through cabinet, especially the Leadership Code. The bills would be returned to me on rather flimsy and ambiguous grounds, for example that more research was needed but without specifically pointing out the areas that they felt were lacking.

The Leadership Code was deferred four times until I told the cabinet that since I had noticed that they did not want to pass this law, I was going to tell Ugandans and our development partners that the cabinet is not interested in fighting corruption. I had really lost patience and was prepared to call a press conference and announce that the government was not ready to fight corruption. That's when the cabinet reluctantly accepted the bill, hoping and praying that it would be rejected by Parliament. I vividly remember two ministers laughing at me and saying that though I had 'blackmailed' them into approving the bill to go to Parliament, they were sure it would not be passed into law.

Incidentally, I noted that the usual talk that women are less corrupt and more readily accountable and transparent does not appear to be true in Uganda's case. I faced a lot of resistance from my fellow women in the fight against corruption. I remember very well that female ministers gave me a harder time than the males. One particular long-serving and high-profile female minister gave me such a hard time during the discussion of the Leadership Code that she was singularly responsible for referring back the bill to my office three times. I remember confronting her during one discussion of the bill in cabinet and telling her that I was fed up with her attitude towards corruption. I asked her why she was more bent on protecting the corrupt than fighting them. I was so baffled by her stance on corruption that I decided to find out more about her. I came to learn that she was a very wealthy woman with many properties in the city. Alas, I wonder just how she amassed all that wealth!

For one reason or another, throughout my struggle, I did not get support from female ministers, especially those holding full cabinet positions. Even in my struggle for land rights for women, I was denounced by my fellow women ministers, including the then Vice President herself, Hon Dr Specioza Wandira Kazibwe, when I tried to resurrect the defeated land co-ownership clause and put up a spirited fight once again in its defence, as detailed in a previous chapter.

## The Fight Against My Ministry Turns Personal

As we continued with our struggle against corruption, the battles between the Minister for Justice on one side and the IGG, and myself on the other went on. In one of the procurement cases that we were investigating in the Electoral Commission, Hon Janat Mukwaya accused the IGG and I of sabotage and reported us to the Prime Minister, Proffesor Apollo Nsibambi. When the Prime Minister summoned us, we stood our ground, saying that the contract in question was not to be signed until all the investigations were complete.

The minister escalated the issue further by taking it to the President, who called a meeting at State House between the minister and the IGG, but left me out. The President prevailed over the IGG and allowed the procurement contract to proceed. That particular contract for the purchase of electronic voter machines was later to cause the government a financial loss of two billion Ugandan shillings.

Despite that setback, we never wavered in our efforts. We continued our attempts to dig deeper into the activities of the Electoral Commission by instituting a grand investigation, which eventually resulted in the disbanding

184 The Struggle for Freedom & Democracy Betrayed

of the Aziz Kasujja-led Commission. This intensified Hon Janat Mukwaya's resentment of the IGG and myself. She was determined to fight back to protect the Electoral Commission and her ministry staff, particularly Lucien Tibaruha.

In revenge, the minister started 'creatively' compiling a dossier about me to prove that I was the most corrupt minister and therefore had no moral authority to fight corruption. In one cabinet meeting, she presented information to the effect that I was involved in corruption through influence-peddling and fraud. I happened to be out of the country at that time. In my absence, she told cabinet that I had coerced the Electoral Commission to employ my children under fictitious Kiganda names, and as such, I was not a proper and fit person to lead the Ministry of Ethics and Integrity. The chair of cabinet that day, Hon Moses Ali, the 2nd Deputy Prime Minister, rightly decided that since I was not present to respond to her allegations, she should wait and present her accusations when I was present.

Towards the general elections of 2001, my two sons, Gideon and Gilbert responded to an Electoral Commission advert for temporary work at the commission. Gideon had completed his course at Makerere University, while Gilbert was in his long vacation after completing A Level. My sons, alongside some of their friends, managed to get the temporary jobs, which I am told were on first-come first-served basis. At that time I was out of the country and only learnt that they were now working at the Electoral Commission after I had returned. Incidentally, my children – Gideon Magembe Matembe and Gilbert Mayanja Matembe – carry Kiganda names so it gave the schemers a soft spot to attack because they probably could not believe that the Kiganda names that my sons hold are their genuine names.

On my return, I was told about these absurd accusations. Unfortunately, at the next cabinet meeting, in which I intended to submit my defence and quash those allegations, Hon Janat Mukwaya was not present; she had travelled out of the country. The matter dragged on for a while until the Prime Minister, Right Hon Proffessor Apollo Nsibambi, promised to handle it.

Unknown to me, the Prime Minister passed the issue on to the IGG for investigation. One day, my son Gideon, aged only 20 at that time, called to tell me that he had been summoned by the IGG to answer some questions. He had been asked to take with him his birth certificate and that of Gilbert, his brother. He asked me, "Mummy, what is happening? Does the IGG think that I am a thief?" He sounded so depressed and hurt at the thought of being wanted by the IGG for questioning.

"Take it easy, my son. Just go there and answer all the questions truthfully," I said to him.

Gideon went for the meeting and answered all the questions honestly. When the IGG submitted his report to Right Hon Proffessor Apollo Nsibambi, it showed that Hon Janat Mukwaya's wild allegations contained not a single iota of truth. The Prime Minister called both of us to his office to discuss the matter. Hon Janat Mukwaya swallowed a humble pie and apologised to me and I forgave her. However, I told her that I did not know that office matters could reach such an extent of personal hatred as to involve my innocent young children. I was deeply hurt by that incident, but I forgave her and continued on with the struggle against corruption.

Besides Hon Mukwaya, many other cabinet colleagues hated my guts. I tend to believe that as champagne was popped at the *Red Pepper* offices after I lost my ministerial position, more champagne must have been popped by some ministers, especially Hon Janat Mukwaya, who I believe could not wait to see me exiting the cabinet door.

## President Museveni Shoots the Leadership Code Act in the Foot

By all means, manoeuvres or otherwise, President Museveni has over time proved that he is not committed to fighting corruption at all. On the contrary, it is indeed accurate to say that corruption and patronage together form the fuel of the engine that runs President Museveni's NRM government. Throughout my tenure as minister, this cover-up and shielding of the corrupt and the sheer unwillingness to fight corruption can be best illustrated by the disgraceful way in which President Museveni shot the Leadership Code in the foot.

The Leadership Code was conceived as a law that would be critical in fighting corruption. **Article 233(1) of the Constitution provides that "Parliament shall by law establish a Leadership Code of Conduct for persons**

**holding such offices as may be specified by Parliament",** and Article 234 vests the powers to enforce the Leadership Code of Conduct in the IGG "or such other authority as Parliament may by law prescribe". Section 1(2) of the Constitution (Consequential Provisions) Act, 1995, provides that until Parliament prescribes any other authority to be responsible for enforcing the Leadership Code of Conduct, the IGG shall be responsible for enforcing it.

Specified leaders who are bound by the provisions of the Code include the President, the Vice President, the Speaker of Parliament, the Prime Minister, ministers, members of parliament, judges and magistrates, permanent secretaries, directors, presidential advisors, ambassadors and high commissioners, the Governor of the Bank of Uganda and heads of departments of the bank, constitutional commissioners, the Auditor General, the Inspector General of Government, vice-chancellors of government-controlled universities, chairpersons of districts and district councillors, and top civil servants of local governments.

Section 4(1)(b) of the Act requires every leader to submit a written declaration of his or her income, assets and liabilities once every two years during the month of March to the IGG. Section 4(8) of the Act provides that a leader who fails without reasonable cause to submit a declaration of his or her income, assets and liabilities to the IGG commits a breach of the Code, and the penalty for this breach under Section 35(b) of the Act is dismissal from or vacation of office.

In essence, the Leadership Code Act had the broad purpose of curbing corruption by discouraging the illicit acquisition of wealth since the law required that every leader's assets, income and wealth are periodically declared to see how they were acquired in relation to one's income.

One of the first offenders of the Leadership Code Act was Major Kakooza Mutale, who was a Special Presidential Advisor/Assistant in charge of political affairs. He was responsible for the infamous Kalangala Action Plan mentioned in the earlier chapters of this book. In accordance with the provisions of the Code, in May 2003, the IGG wrote to the President and recommended the termination of Major Kakooza Mutale's employment, after he breached the Leadership Code Act by failing to declare his wealth. The President acted and terminated Major Kakooza Mutale's employment.

After the termination of his employment, Major Kakooza Mutale went to court to sue the IGG in the case: *Roland Kakooza Mutale v. the Attorney General Application No. 665 of 2003 arising out of HCCA No. 40 of 2003*. His main argument in this petition was that there was no prescribed legal form on which to declare his wealth. Many lawyers and other commentators indeed argued that it was a mere technicality since other leaders had been able to declare their wealth in various forms.

In an absurd twist of events, President Museveni on 22nd September, 2003, swore an affidavit in support of Major Kakooza Mutale against the IGG, claiming that he dismissed him because he was 'ordered' to do so by the IGG, although he would have preferred to retain him.

*"AFFIDAVIT*

*I, YOWERI KAGUTA MUSEVENI, c/o State House, P. O. Box 25497, KAMPALA do solemnly swear and state as follows: -*

1. *That I am a male adult Ugandan of sound mind and the President of Uganda.*

2. *That on the 6th August 2003, I relieved Major Roland Kakooza Mutale of his duties as a Presidential Advisor solely and exclusively on the basis of the recommendation of the Inspector General of Government [IGG] and not for any other reason.*

3. *That the IGG advised me that he had made his recommendation to me to relieve Major Roland Kakooza Mutale of his duties having carried out all the necessary legal inquiries and that according to the Leadership Code I, as the Appointing Authority, had no choice in the matter but simply to carry out the statutory duty of implementing the recommendation of the IGG.*

4. *That I therefore relieved Major Roland Kakooza Mutale of his duties on the basis of the IGG's recommendation and having been given the impression that all the correct legal principles and procedures had been fulfilled, and all steps taken to ensure that he gets fair treatment according to natural justice.*

5. *That if the Court finds that the IGG made the above stated recommendation to me on the basis of a flawed procedure and never followed the Leadership Code and the law generally in making his recommendation,*

*I am prepared to reinstate Major Kakooza Mutale to his Office as Presidential Advisor.*

6. *That I make this affidavit in certification of the facts laid hereinabove.*

7. *That whatever is stated herein is true to the best of my knowledge save Par.3 which is true based on the advice and information to me by the IGG.*

*Sworn at Kisozi}*
*By the said YOWERI KAGUTA MUSEVENI} signed*
*This 22nd day of September 200 } DEPONENT*
*Before me:*
*signed*
*A Commissioner for Oaths"*

In his affidavit, President Museveni swore: "That the IGG advised me that he had made his recommendation to me to relieve Major Roland Kakooza Mutale of his duties having carried out all the necessary legal inquiries and that according to the Leadership Code, I, as the Appointing Authority, had no choice in the matter but simply to carry out the statutory duty of implementing the recommendation of the IGG." In the same affidavit, Museveni swore that: "...if the Court finds out that the IGG made the...recommendation to me on the basis of a flawed procedure and never followed the Leadership Code and the law generally in making his recommendation, I am prepared to reinstate Major Roland Kakooza Mutale to his Office as Presidential Advisor."

On the basis of this affidavit, the court ruled against the IGG, saying that he had no powers to order the Head of State. Consequently, Major Kakooza Mutale was reinstated to his position.

My concern is that if the President was truly committed to fighting corruption, how could he of all people, be the one to defend someone who had violated a code that had been put in place to fight corruption? In my mind, Museveni's affidavit sent a clear signal that him and his government were not interested in fighting political corruption and were further entrenching the notion that the IGG's duty was but a thankless task. Such acts did not only create laxity but also demoralised the entire service chain of those who are supposed to act against corrupt individuals.

The Office of the President did not stop there. They made sure that the Leadership Code Act was decimated and nullified. Fox Odoi, a legal assistant to the President at that time, alongside James Akampumuza lodged a petition – *Fox Odoi Oywelowo & James Akampumuza v. Attorney General, Constitutional Petition No 8 of 2003,* challenging various sections of the Leadership Code Act as being inconsistent with certain articles of the Constitution of Uganda, with a view that the Leadership Code Act should therefore be declared a nullity. Without shame, President Museveni once again supplied affidavit evidence in support of the petition. This to me was yet another blatant display of lack of political will to fight corruption and, in fact, an abdication of the President's duty and obligation to fight corruption.

In this petition of Fox Odoi Oywelowo and James Akampumuza versus the Attorney General, the Constitutional Court held that sections 19(1), 20(1), and 35(b) and (d) of the Leadership Code Act were null and void in respect to presidential appointees because they were inconsistent with laid down procedures in the Constitution for disciplining such appointees, and the same sections fettered the discretion vested in the President by the Constitution in the disciplining of his or her appointees. Basically, that the Act did not give the President discretion in punishing the officers who had breached the Leadership Code.

Effectively, the recommendations of the Inspectorate today no longer bind the President. He need not implement them. That court ruling was a blow to the fight against corruption. Not only did the decision in that case cripple the enforcement of the Leadership Code because presidential appointees are the main leaders in this country, it also greatly damaged and undermined the authority of the IGG in the public domain. The IGG became merely a barking dog when it came to requiring the President to implement the recommendations made by the Inspectorate. In essence, it was deeply frustrating that the fight against corruption was left in the hands of an institution whose recommendations were no longer binding.

Further, in 2005, Parliament made an amendment to the Constitution under Chapter 14 – Article 235A - establishing a Leadership Code Tribunal "whose composition, jurisdiction and functions shall be prescribed by Parliament" although Article 234 of the Constitution vesting powers of enforcement in the IGG was not changed. In 2017, Parliament amended the Leadership Code Act, 2002 putting the Leadership Code (Amendment) Act, 2017 in place. The amendment gave effect to Article 235A of the constitution by providing for the establishment, composition, jurisdiction and functions of the Leadership code tribunal so as to strengthen the enforcement of the code and other related matters.

However, by the end of 2018, the Executive was yet to establish the Leadership Code Tribunal. Again this has had a crippling effect on the operationalisation of the code and the overall effectiveness of the IG. Again, such delays illustrate the lack of political will to fight corruption that stems right from the very apex of Uganda's leadership and ripples down through the various institutions.

## Reluctance to Empower the Office of the IGG

Besides the issues with the enforceability of the Leadership Code Act amidst nullifications of particular clauses by the courts of law, the institution of the IGG remained with limited capacity to carry out its mandate. The IGG's office is the foremost government body charged with eliminating corruption. However, it is disheartening that such a pivotal institution in the fight against corruption was not fully constituted for more than ten years after the amendment of the IGG Act. The President was apparently reluctant to fully constitute the office of the IGG and this hampered the ability and effectiveness of the office. In fact, it was once sued and challenged as having no powers to prosecute because it had not been fully constituted.

In the case, *Jim Muhwezi & 3 Ors v Attorney General & Anor (Constitutional Petition No.10 of 2008)*, Jim Muhwezi filed a constitutional petition challenging the independence of the IGG, Justice Faith Mwondha. The 1st petitioner, Jim Muhwezi, was at the time an MP for Rukungiri Municipality and a former Minister for Health, while the 2nd respondent, Captain Mike Mukula and 3rd respondent, Dr Alex Kamugisha were at the material time State Ministers for Health. The 4th respondent, Alice Kaboyo was a staffer at State House employed as Private Secretary to the President.

Available court records show that in October 2007, the four respondents were charged at Buganda Road Chief Magistrates Court of various offences of abuse of office, theft, embezzlement, causing financial loss, making false documents, forgery and uttering false documents all in connection with Global Alliance for Vaccines and Immunization (GAVI) Funds which were donor funds being administered by the Ministry of Health. The charges were preferred after the IGG had made a report to the President implicating the four respondents in the misuse of the funds. It was the IGG who had investigated the case on orders of the President and it was that office conducting the prosecutions in the aforementioned case.

At the trial, the respondents pleaded not guilty and objected to being prosecuted by the IGG on the grounds that it would be unconstitutional for that office to prosecute them. They obtained a court order staying the proceedings until the constitutionality of the proposed trial was determined by the Constitutional Court. They filed this petition seeking for the following remedies:-

(a) A declaration that the arrest and prosecution by the Inspector General of Government of your petitioners with offences other than offences mentioned in article 230(1) was and is in contravention of and ultra vires the powers conferred upon the IGG under article 230(1) of the Constitution of the Republic of Uganda 1995.

(b) A declaration that the arrest and prosecution of your petitioners by the IGG for the offences mentioned herein above was and continues to be done without authority or legal basis and in contravention of the supreme law of the land and is unconstitutional to the extent that it is inconsistent with and contravenes the provisions of Article 230(1) of the 1995 Constitution.

(c) A declaration that the act of arresting and prosecuting your petitioners by the IGG with offences for which the IGG has no authority to arrest and/or prosecute anyone is illegal, ultra vires the powers conferred upon the IGG under the Constitution and is nullity.

(d) An order that the prosecution of your petitioners be discontinued for being ultra vires and inconsistent with and in contravention of the Constitution of the Republic of Uganda.

Jim Muhwezi swore an affidavit where he claimed that Justice Mwondha, a judge of the High Court was holding the Office of the IGG contrary to the principle of separation of powers and independence of the Judiciary.

Furthermore, according to the Act, the Office of the IGG would be fully constituted with a substantive head and two deputies, but for over ten years, the office had the head (IGG) but only one deputy IGG. Also, for about two years, the office of the IGG was left in limbo to operate with neither a substantive head nor the two substantive deputies. This also goes a long way to demonstrate that the President has only paid lip service to the fight against corruption.

It was perhaps because of the above circumstances that three ministers: Sam Kutesa, Eng John Nasasira and Mwesigwa Rukutana challenged the Attorney General in the Constitutional Court in the case, *Hon Sam Kutesa & 2 Others Vs Attorney General, Constitutional Petition No. 46 of 2011 and Constitutional Petition No. 54 of 2011, arising from the Anti-Corruption Court at Kololo Criminal Case N0. 184 of 2011.*

Available court records show that, Hon Sam Kutesa, Hon John Nasasira and Hon Mwesigwa Rukutana, the "petitioner/applicants", and all ministers at the time in the Uganda Government were jointly charged, at the instance of the IGG, with the offences of abuse of office and causing financial loss **C/s 11 and 20** of the Anti-Corruption Act, before the Chief Magistrate, Anti-Corruption Court, Kampala, on 13th October, 2011 in Criminal case No.184 of 2011. Each petitioner pleaded not guilty to the charges and was subsequently released on bail with stringent conditions being attached.

Also, at the instance and prayer of both the petitioners, and the IGG as prosecutor, the Anti-Corruption Chief Magistrate's Court, on 24.10.2011, referred to the Constitutional Court four questions for interpretation. The court also stayed the criminal proceedings before it in the case, pending resolution of the four questions as below:

1. Whether the IGG can prosecute or cause prosecution in respect of cases involving corruption, abuse of authority or of public office under Article 230 of the Constitution of the Republic of Uganda, when it is not duly constituted in accordance with Article 223(2) of the Constitution and Section 3 (2) of the Inspectorate of Government Act to consist of the IGG and two Deputy IGGs.

2. Whether Section 49 of the Anti-Corruption Act, 2009, which gives powers of prosecution to the IGG is inconsistent or in contravention of Article 230(1) of the Constitution, which gives prosecution powers to the IG.

3. Whether committal proceedings by magistrates in the Anti-Corruption Division and cancellation of bail under Section 168(4) of the Magistrates Courts Act do not violate Article 23 of the Constitution of the Republic of Uganda, which provides for protection of personal liberty, especially in view of section 51 of the Anti-Corruption Act, 2009, which

gives special jurisdiction to the magistrates in the Anti-Corruption Division.

4. Whether Article 137(5) of the Constitution which denies the original court the exercise of the discretionary powers, is in contravention and inconsistent with Article 128 of the Constitution, which provides for the independence of the judiciary.

The Constitutional court ruled that: "The Inspectorate of Government cannot, through the Inspector General of Government, when he/she is the only one in office, prosecute or cause prosecution in respect of cases involving corruption, abuse of authority or public office under Article 230 of the Constitution, when the Inspectorate of Government is not duly constituted in accordance with Article 223(2) of the Constitution and Section 3 (2) of the Inspectorate of Government Act No.5 of 2002, which require the Inspectorate to consist of the Inspector General of Government and two Deputy Inspectors General. This declaration is to act prospectively and not retrospectively as from the date of delivery of this judgement."

Therefore all these corruption cases involving powerful ministers of government were dismissed because of the failure of the President to fully constitute the office of the IGG which is responsible to fight corruption.

## President Museveni's Refusal to Heed the Advice of the Minister for Ethics and Integrity and the Recommendations of the IGG

When the IGG and my office advised the President, he often did not take our considered advice at all or seriously. One such example was the case of Mr Lucien Tibaruha. We advised the President against appointing Mr Tibaruha as Solicitor General because he was involved in dubious dealings with government contracts, but the President decided to ignore good advice and went ahead to appoint him for reasons best known to himself.

From several of our investigations, we had found out that Mr Lucien Tibaruha used to connive with people entering into contracts with government. His office would deliberately draft poor contracts with obvious loopholes that favoured the shoddy contractors against the government. Thereafter, he would turn around and advise the contractors to sue government and be compensated large sums of money, which he would probably share with them. Through such double dealing, the government lost billions of shillings. All these investigations were well documented. They could have been another reason why Hon Janat Mukwaya fought the IGG, since the Solicitor General's office falls under the Ministry of Justice.

As a matter of fact, in 2004 when former IGG, now Justice Jotham Tumwesigye, ordered the arrest of Lucien Tibaruha, then Ag Solicitor General, President Museveni personally accused the IGG of frustrating his government's programs. I remember that Mr Tibaruha's arrest had been ordered by the IGG after he irregularly sanctioned the payment of thirteen billion shillings to one James Musinguzi Garuga in compensation for his farm which government had allocated to settlers.

Long after Jotham Tumwesigye had left the IGG post and Justice Faith Mwondha was appointed the IGG, Tibaruha as Solicitor General continued with his unscrupulous schemes. When Mwondha raised similar complaints against Mr Tibaruha, the President praised Mwondha as a fantastic IGG because she had netted Mr Tibaruha and exposed his schemes. This was strange to us because we had already advised the President against Tibaruha, but he had dismissed our good advice.

However, with President Museveni, as long as you are a good 'cadre', you cannot be charged with corruption. So I suspect that Mr Tibaruha had probably stepped on some big fellows' toes and fallen out of favour and that was when the President's eyes opened to his dubious dealings that we had earlier warned about.

## Advice Against the Appointment of Sam Rwakoojo to the Electoral Commission

Another case in which President Museveni disregarded the advice of state institutions was in the appointment of Sam Rwakoojo as Secretary to the Electoral Commission. The Public Service Commission, alongside my ministry, had objected to this appointment for two main reasons: he was not qualified to take up the position and he was connected to a supplies company of the Electoral Commission.

First, the position of Secretary of the Electoral Commission is equivalent to a Permanent Secretary of a ministry. At that time, the prerequisite for becoming a PS was that the candidate had to sit and pass a merit-based exam/interview. Sam Rwakoojo had neither sat for such an interview nor had he done similar work before, therefore he had not qualified for the position.

Secondly, Sam Rwakoojo was involved with the Electoral Commission as a supplier. In close collaboration with Hon Sam Kutesa, he was connected to Lithotec, a South African-based company that supplied printed electoral materials such as ballot papers and the like to the EC. This was a clear case of conflict of interest. However, the President ignored our advice and prevailed over the Electoral Commission to appoint Sam Rwakoojo against the technical advice of the Public Service Commission and my office.

## Presidential Pardon to the Corrupt

I must mention that it is extremely difficult to investigate and successfully prosecute cases of corruption because gathering evidence and finding witnesses who are willing to testify in court is such a painstaking activity. Nevertheless, my office and that of the IGG managed to successfully investigate, prosecute and cause the conviction of some high-profile individuals. It was so heartbreaking and demoralizing, however, that after finally netting the corrupt and having them sentenced in court, the president would turn around and negate all our efforts by exercising his privilege to grant presidential pardon to the convicted plunderers of government finances. It sent a terribly negative signal to the public. Here he was as president posturing that he would catch the corrupt and deal with them, and yet whenever the responsible institutions managed to net a big fish, the President turned around and set the convict free, thus going against his own word. I personally believe that such unwarranted presidential pardons serve to abet corruption. That was the exact opposite of the signal the government ought to be sending out, which is that corruption is a high-risk misadventure.

For instance, there was the case, *Mulindwa Birimumaso Vs Government Central Purchasing Corporation Hccs 674/98, [2004] 348 Kalr (Reported)* of Hon Mulindwa Birimumaso who was convicted for corruption but the President forgave him.

There was the case of the Permanent Secretary, Prof Gastavus Ssenyonga and Under Secretary, Ms Christine Namudu Kigundu of the Ministry of Agriculture. In the case, *Prof Gastavus Ssenyonga &Anoer v Uganda ((Cr. Application No.12 Of 1999)) [1999] UGCA 16,* they were both convicted for causing financial loss and abuse of office and sentenced to 7 years in jail, before the President intervened and pardoned them.

Another case in point was when the President worked so hard to save Nathan Muhanguzi, an LC III Chairman of Rwanyamahembe sub-county in Kashari, Mbarara District. The chairman had been accused of swindling over twenty million shillings from the local sub-county, and he was caught. There was sufficient evidence against him, and so he was arrested and jailed. The case came to me and his supporters wanted him to be set free, which I refused. That LC III Chairman eventually got access to Mrs Jovia Saleh and her sister Kellen Kayonga, who, as I have since learnt, wanted this man to unseat Hon John Kazoora in Kashari; so they took him to see Museveni at his home in Rwakitura. The two sisters told the President that Matembe and Kazoora were persecuting this man because he was a strong NRM supporter and they asked the President to intervene. So His Excellency invited the chairman of the district,who by then was Fred Kamugira, Hon Kazoora and myself to Rwakitura, and asked us what was going on with the LC III Chairman of Rwanyamahembe? And, by the way, the chairman was there too.

We talked about the case and presented all the facts and the LC III Chairman also presented his case. It was really clear from the evidence that there was no alternative but for the chairman to face the case of corruption. We parted company after the President had told the chairman that he would face the courts of law because he had not been able to exonerate himself.

About three weeks later, the President called me and the then Director of Public Prosecutions (DPP), Mr Richard Butera, to his office at State House and said, "You know, Hon Matembe, I have called you here and also Richard, the DPP, to see how we can sort out this case of the Chairman LC III of Rwanyamahembe; to see whether the case can be withdrawn."

The President told me that he had talked to the DPP about how to withdraw this case from the courts, but Mr Butera had said that since I was the chair of the Anti-Corruption Inter-Agency Forum, I knew the stage at which each case had reached, and therefore he could not withdraw the case without my knowledge.

I said, "Sir, of course the DPP has unlimited powers, and he works under nobody's control; he can withdraw any case at whichever stage it is, as and when he chooses. But since you made me the Minister for Ethics and Integrity, we, together with all the agencies that are involved in fighting corruption, formed an inter-agency forum to coordinate our work on all the corruption cases so that we can follow every case and know what is happening at whatever stage, and why such action has been taken. Therefore Mr Butera was right to involve me in this discussion, but he has all the legal powers to do what he wants and I have no right to stop him from withdrawing the case. But as for me, I strongly object to the withdrawal and if it is done, I will make a public statement about it."

This was really a small sub-county case that the President should not have got involved in. But he did because when it comes to political support, the President will forgive the corrupt, so long as they continue to give him political support. Museveni perceived the case as one in which he could lose his political support in Rwanyamahembe, Kashari County. Of course, when I was removed from office the case was dropped and the man went scot free.

## President Museveni Becomes Hostage to Corruption and the Corrupt

President Museveni's motto is really simple and straight forward: You are only corrupt if you are not a 'cadre' or his supporter. As long as you are a cadre but you are corrupt, he simply closes an eye. This reveals a huge contradiction between what he says and what he actually practices. Perhaps, as Jesus says in the Bible, the 'spirit is willing but the body is weak'. Maybe the spirit of the President is willing to fight corruption, but because he loves power so much, he cannot fight the corrupt because the corrupt are the ones keeping him in power. He cannot do away with them, so he has become hostage to corruption and the corrupt. The Kinyankore proverb: *Ekyokunda kikunagisa ekyokwaitse*, which means that longing after an object of your desire will make you lose what you already possess, aptly sums up Museveni's dilemma. His obsession with power made him lose all the values he had originally started with because values such as fighting corruption stand in the way of his retaining power.

As it is now, corruption is the engine that sustains the President in power. Corruption has become a legitimate way of life for the NRM, considering the fact that the President has no shame in moving around with sacks of money to dish out to naïve Ugandans.

Look at the bribery of MPs whenever he wants a certain bill passed or a decision which is not in the people's interest made. Consider all these jobs of RDCs, presidential advisors and many others,which are dished out with reckless abandon to anyone who dares to make some noise against the government. The corrupt patronage system has totally undermined the true tenets of democracy and good governance in Uganda. In elections these days, the choice of leaders no longer depends on the ideas, ability and capacity of the candidate, but on how much one can pay in exchange for the vote. How terribly sad!

# Chapter Eleven

# My Work with Hon Janet K Museveni, the First Lady

## My First Encounter with Mrs Janet Museveni

I remember the first time I met Mrs Janet Museveni was around 1979, after the overthrow of Amin, during the UNLF government. She may not remember that occasion, but we met at my home in Port Bell. She had come with her friend, Mrs Alice Kakwano, who our family knows very well. They came to see my husband because they wanted to buy beer. By then Museveni was the Minister of Defence, while my husband was a brewer at Uganda Breweries in Port Bell.

At that time there was a desperate scarcity of beer, sodas and other similar commodities. The scarcity was so dire that many people used to forge all sorts of invitation cards for functions such as baptisms and weddings because if you had a function, you stood a good chance of getting an allocation for beer from the breweries and sugar or soda from the factories.

Owing to the scarcity of such essential items, *magendo*– Kiswahili for the smuggling and illegal trade in essential items on the black market–thrived. My husband was not responsible for the allocation of beer; his responsibility was to brew the beer and declare it to the sales department. Nevertheless, because he worked at Uganda Breweries, many people who wanted beer and knew him would come to seek his assistance in getting them an allocation. I guess that is the reason why Mrs Kakwano brought Mrs Museveni to see my husband.

Because of this scarcity, some people used to secure allocation chits for beer from the bosses at Uganda Breweries, such as the MD, Marketing Manager and Sales Manager under the pretext that they had a social function. In turn, they would go and re-sell the beer on the black market at heavily-inflated prices. So many people engaged in *magendo*, got rich and built mansions. Though my husband had access to some of these products that were in high demand, he was never involved in the illegal sale of beer. And I used to nag him that we were dying of poverty while other people made money out of the beer he brewed and had easy access to. Looking back, I am now glad that he never engaged in *magendo*. And because of his integral worth, we have property of high value and a retirement home, courtesy of Uganda Breweries.

I do not know the reason why these two ladies wanted beer; whether they had a function or otherwise. Anyway, I welcomed them into our home and called my husband to come and see his guests. He came from his office and talked to them, and I believe he took them to the brewery to introduce them to one or more of the big bosses.

I didn't find out whether they had achieved their mission. At that time, I had recently got a job as a lecturer in law at the Uganda College of Commerce (the current Makerere University Business School). As a fresh graduate, the status gap between these ladies and I was so wide that I personally didn't have much to talk about with them. That was my first encounter with Mrs Janet Museveni.

## Meeting the First Lady

The next time I saw Mrs Janet Museveni, her husband had taken over as President and therefore she was the First Lady of Uganda.

One of her first social initiatives as the First Lady was to found the Uganda Women's Efforts to Save Orphans (UWESO). I was one of the founding members of UWESO, but I did not get close to her then because at that time, my energies and passion were dedicated to the fight for gender equality and women's empowerment, and yet UWESO's main concern was the plight of orphans.

As I have already mentioned in the previous chapters, because of my outspokenness and passion for advocating women and girls' causes, I quickly became nationally noticed for my work. This drew the attention of the First Lady and she eventually invited me to meet her in 1989. I had just been elected to the NRC (the equivalent of Parliament then), as the Woman Representative for Mbarara District. I had also been appointed a commissioner on the Uganda Constitutional Commission. I was extremely surprised, however, when her personal assistant informed me that the First Lady wanted to have an urgent meeting with me.

At State House, I had a long chat with the First Lady. She asked me my details and showed a keen interest in getting to know me. I noticed that she didn't remember my previous encounter with her at my house in the days of *magendo*. Anyway, she said she sought me out because she wanted me to represent her in Minneapolis, Minnesota, where she had been invited in her capacity as the founder and patron of UWESO.

I felt that her request was too daunting a task for me. I nevertheless thanked her for the favour and the confidence she had in me, but told her that I was quite scared to take on the assignment. I said, "Madam, first of all, I don't think I'm the right person for this assignment because I have not yet attained the high profile to fit in your shoes. Secondly, although I am a member of UWESO, I am not involved in its day-to-day work and I don't know much about its programs because my main commitment and interest is in the issues of gender equality and women's empowerment, and therefore most of my civil society work has been with Action for Development (ACFODE)."

She told me not to worry about that because I would

be assisted by Diana Lule, the then chairperson of UWESO, who was competent and conversant with issues of UWESO. She said my role would be to project the political and public profile of Uganda. Although my big mouth causes me trouble sometimes, it has also enhanced my profile and enabled me to reach greater heights, like in this case. Mrs Museveni had no reservations at all about my ability to articulate the issues well and be the mouthpiece to give Uganda and UWESO a positive political profile.

I told her that I had yet another challenge. I was not familiar with international travel as this would be but my third trip outside the country. I had made my first two trips out of Uganda in quick succession. My maiden journey and first time on a plane had been in 1988 when I attended the World Congress of Women in Moscow. I was then the Vice Chairperson of Nakawa Division and was part of a team that included Hon Janat Mukwaya, who was then the Director for Women's affairs at the NRM Secretariat; Mrs Florence Nekyon, the then Secretary General of the National Council of Women for Non-Governmental Organizations of Uganda; and the late Zeridah Rwabusyagara, who was the District Administrator (the equivalent of RDC then) of Mubende. When I returned from Moscow, ACFODE nominated me to participate in an Eastern and Southern Africa seminar for women and politics in Harare, Zimbabwe. At that time, I was also the Legal Advisor to ACFODE.

I reiterated my fears about my lack of experience in international travel which made me unsuitable to represent the First Lady. I even suggested that she choose from some of the female ministers then, who included Hon Victoria Ssekitoleko, Hon Joyce Mpanga, Hon Rhoda Kalema and others. But she insisted that I must go. "For me, I have chosen you. You are my best choice. Please go and prepare your speech. We shall review it together."

I was very excited but also unsure about going all the way to America. Nevertheless, I prepared the speech and when she read through, she was comfortable with it.

## Up close and Personal Interaction with President Museveni

Meanwhile, while I was at State House for my meeting with the First Lady, the President was taking a walk in the garden. He saw my small Nissan violet car parked in the lot, and approached my driver and asked whose vehicle it was. I understand that after learning that I was around, he told the guards to inform me not to go before he had met me. As I was leaving after my meeting with the First Lady, I found one of President Museveni's aides waiting for me at the reception. He told me the President wanted to see me and he took me to the President's office. This was a great surprise to me; I was not in the least prepared to have a one-on-one personal conversation with the President.

In his office, President Museveni greeted me and asked me to tell him about myself. I told him everything and was amazed that he knew many people from my place of birth - Rutooma, Kashari. He also knew my father. He asked me what I had been doing all this time. I told him that I was a mobiliser, and had moved through all ladders of leadership from RC 1 to 5 up to the Parliament.

I also got an opportunity to thank him for putting the woman question high up on the Movement agenda. I told him that I was committed to mobilise for the Movement and ready to do my best, especially in the area of women's rights and empowerment.

Although that was my first one-on-one meeting with the President, I had met him earlier at his home in Rwakitura where I was left a bit disappointed that he could not put a face to my name. In 1989 after I had been elected to Parliament, there was an outbreak of foot-and-mouth disease in western Uganda and we were invited as leaders from the region to discuss the issue. Whenever someone put up his hand to speak, the President called up the person by name. When I put up my hand, he simply said, "Yes, Mrs. . . ." I had to tell him my name. He was surprised that it was me. He thought I was Ruhanga-Arinda who worked at the NRM Secretariat. Despite my disappointment that the President didn't know me, and yet I had worked so hard for the Movement in the previous four years, still I was encouraged that my reputation had preceded me.

Interestingly enough, just two days after the Rwakitura meeting, Hon Sam Njuba (RIP), who was then the State Minister for Constitutional Affairs, called me to his office and told me that the President had directed him to appoint me to the Uganda Constitutional Commission. He also asked me if I preferred being a minister or a member of the Constitutional Commission.

"There is nothing I would prefer better than being on the Uganda Constitutional Commission," I told him. What had driven me to politics was to get a platform to espouse the case for gender equality and women empowerment. Now that I was presented with the rare opportunity to participate in drafting a constitution that would work for women, I could not let it go. Here was a golden chance for me to challenge the old laws that were unresponsive and repulsive to women and I embraced it without any hesitation.

The personal interaction with the President at State House came about two weeks after I had been appointed as Commissioner on the Constitutional Commission. Therefore it also presented a perfect opportunity for me to thank him for appointing me to such an important and historic commission. When I tell people that I was appointed to the Uganda Constitutional Commission on merit alone, without any prior relation to or discussion with the President, most do not believe it, especially because of the patronage system that has now taken over President Museveni's government.

At our meeting, the President told me that his wife was getting so many invitations to national and international conferences and other events. He said that he had advised her to find some brilliant and competent women who could, from time to time, represent her at the functions because he didn't want her to become too common. He said that he was glad she had chosen me for this particular trip.

That was my first time to interact closely with both the

President and the First Lady. From that time, we became close, and I believe I was one of the favourites, in terms of work, of both the President and his wife. The First Lady and I really connected and became close. We grew so fond of each other. I really loved her and I believed she loved me too. She trusted and believed in me and as such, she delegated me to attend a number of meetings, conferences and seminars on her behalf.

Quite often, the President and the First Lady would both require my services at the same time. In fact, when I would sometimes be away on an assignment for the First Lady, the President would call my home looking to send me somewhere too, and my husband would tell him that, "She isn't here. Your wife delegated her to represent her somewhere."

At one time, the President called me to his Kisozi ranch and the meeting took so long and went on beyond midnight, and yet I was supposed to represent the First Lady somewhere else the very next morning. The President asked his aides to take me to spend a night in his son Muhoozi's hut, but I instead asked the guards if they would escort me to Kampala. They said they would if I gave them 'fuel', which I did. I was able to get back to Kampala that night, in time to attend the First Lady's function the next morning. So you can see what a cordial relationship the President and his wife had with me.

Eventually, I learnt from the President that the First Lady used to lobby and pester him to appoint me to a ministerial position. Though I was an effective worker and mobiliser, it took quite some time for me to be appointed to the cabinet. Whenever there was a cabinet reshuffle and I was not included, the President thereafter called me, I imagine, to gauge my mood, and see whether I was disappointed or not. I told the President that I didn't care whether I was a minister or not; all I needed was facilitation to properly mobilise women for their empowerment and development.

One day, as I was coming from a mobilisation meeting in Isingiro, my small car broke down and I got a lift on a lorry ferrying charcoal. This incident was reported in the press and the President read about it. He called to ask what I was doing on a charcoal lorry and I explained my predicament. Then he directed his then Principal Private Secretary Amelia Kyambadde to avail me with fifteen million shillings to purchase a vehicle of my preference - a Mitsubishi double cabin pick-up. Indeed, this vehicle did a lot of work, especially during the 1996 presidential elections.

## Good Times with the First Lady

I became the First Lady's trusted confidante on work-related issues and she always consulted me whenever she had a new project to do. She was very happy with the work I was doing for her.

One profound incident that served to draw us closer and cement my relationship with her was the 1995 Women's Conference in Beijing to mark the Women's Decade. It was puzzling that Hon Specioza Kazibwe, the then Vice President and Minister for Gender, who was in charge, did not deem Hon Winnie Byanyima and I fit to be part of the 100-member government delegation to Beijing, despite the fact that we were outstanding women leaders who were doing a lot to uplift the plight of women in Uganda. People wrote about it in the press, questioning the wisdom of leaving us out of the 100-member government delegation.

However, since we were internationally acclaimed for our activism in the women's movement, Hon Byanyima and I received our invitations straight from the United Nations headquarters in New York. We were on the program to address the NGO forum plenary sessions and I remember Byanyima addressed the plenary in one morning session, while I addressed it that afternoon.

On the evening before I was meant to return to Uganda, I received a call from the PA of the First Lady. I understand they had been frantically looking for me all over Beijing and had even been to the hotel where the Ugandan delegation was staying, but could not find me since I was not part of the official government delegation. The First Lady asked me to stay on because she wanted me to help her work on the speech she was going to present to the conference. When I told her I was scheduled to return to Uganda the next day, she wondered why I was returning home when the conference was just beginning. I told her that I had come specifically to address the NGO forum plenary and was not funded to attend as a government delegate. She wondered how I, of all the people, could have been left out of the government delegation. I actually suggested that she could work with Mrs Joy Kwesiga, who was the chairperson of ACFODE then, but the First Lady insisted that I stay because she wanted to work with me.

In regard to the logistical challenges, she said she would get back to me, and indeed, at midnight I received a call from her. She told me that she would send her PA to pick me up the next day and I went to stay with her in the State Lodge in Beijing. During my stay, we shared a lot together and, in fact, that was the time when I really got close to her. Every evening, we sat in the sitting room and talked about many things. It was also the time when I got to know how close the First Lady was with God. I admired her relationship with God and wished to be like her. Down the road, I eventually became born-again myself, before the end of 1995, and I must admit that her deep knowledge of God played a big role in inspiring me to return to the Lord.

We continued working well together on several projects. I remember clearly that Hon Joyce Mpanga and I worked tooth and nail to assist the First Lady to establish an organisation called the National Strategy for Advancement of Rural Women (NSARW). We worked around the clock and spent months drafting the structure and constitution of NSARW and it successfully started operations. We even assisted in the process of hiring senior staff, including the appointment of Mrs Margaret Kakitahi as the Executive Director. I don't know what became of that organisation later, after the First Lady went into politics and was appointed a minister, but what I know is that initially, NSARW did a lot of work towards the empowerment and advancement of rural women.

Generally, the First Lady has done commendable work in terms of the advancement of women, mainly through NSARW and UWESO. I am proud to say that I was part of that success since I was actively involved in the founding of both those organisations.

Having appreciated my work and passion, the First Lady wanted me to be appointed to a ministerial position. I don't know whether my appointment, finally, was caused by the First Lady's lobbying on my behalf or if it was out of President Museveni's own volition, but what I appreciated most was not merely being appointed a minister but the particular ministry that I was appointed to head. It gave me great honor and a sense of fulfillment to be appointed the pioneer Minister for Ethics and Integrity because it confirmed to me and to others, that I was considered a person of high ethical values and integrity. The appointment showed that when the President chose to establish a ministry for the building of ethical values and to fight against corruption, it was in me that he saw the most suitable person for the task.

## No Longer at Ease with the First Lady

After I had been appointed a minister, the First Lady called me to her home and we had a cup of tea. She told me that she was very happy that I was finally a minister. Like me, she was also particularly excited that I had been given the mantle of fighting corruption and building ethics and integrity in public office.

She told me a story that involved corruption that had

touched her. It was about a woman at Mulago Hospital whose uterus was about to be removed because her documentation had been misplaced and no health worker there would look for it unless they were paid a bribe. Luckily for that woman, someone intervened and her uterus was saved.

The First Lady went on to say that she wanted to join hands with me to fight the scourge of corruption in Uganda. This was music to my ears! It was an indicator that my campaign against corruption would succeed now that I did not only have the good will of the First Lady, but that she was willing to actually join the fight herself.

I was truly exhilarated, and in my characteristic naïve innocence, I told her, "Now that you're joining me to fight corruption, I am confident that we will succeed. In fact, the best place to begin is here – right here in the Office of the President and State House. This is where our fight against corruption must start."

It is very difficult to describe how her face changed in a split second. All of a sudden her countenance switched. If she had been a white person, her face would have turned pale. She stared at me with an open mouth as if I was from Mars, and then she asked, "State House? And the Office of the President? Do you mean here?"

"Yes, madam," I replied. "You know this issue of the Uganda Commercial Bank (UCB)? In fact, I had wanted to meet the President and talk to him about it. People are reporting that Gen Salim Saleh is involved. Also, in other high-profile corruption cases, people are pointing fingers at Hon John Kazoora and Hon Sam Kutesa."

She interjected and asked me which Hon Kazoora I was talking about. I replied that I was talking about the Hon Kazoora from Ntungamo, her uncle and guardian. I added that, "People are also talking about Hon Rukikaire in connection to the UCB issue. They say he knows what is going on." Hon. Rukikaire was at the time the Minister for Privatisation which was handling the sale of UCB. I told her that these were very high-profile people and therefore I needed to tell the President about the cases. I asked her to help me get an immediate appointment with him.

By then, her face had totally changed. She looked at me angrily and said, "*Matembe, naiwe buzima ori omu bibi bya'bairu na'bahima? Hatishi nyowe obunkweta ohurire, biri naiwe obaire ofire?*" Meaning, Matembe, are you also involved in this nonsense of the Bairu against the Bahima? I thought you were a sensible person whom I could confide in, but it seems you are also hopeless and useless."

I was so shocked and dumbfounded, and I asked her how the issue of the Bairu and Bahima (historical rivalry between the two sub-groups of the Banyankore) had come into the matter.

She answered, "You can't be serious; you mean you want to waste Mzee's time with this nonsense? All this while, I thought you were someone of substance, but you're just like those who are involved in that nonsense of persecuting the Bahima. Look at the names you have given me: Kazoora, Kutesa, Salim Saleh, Rukikaire. Don't you see?"

That was very shocking to me. I said, "I am very sorry, mama. I didn't intend to appear like that because the issue of the Bairu and Bahima has never been part of my life even as I grew up. After all, I come from Kashaari where we are a combination of both."

She went on, "How does Uncle Kazoora come into this? And Kutesa? What about Salim Saleh? These are people who sacrificed a lot for this country!"

I was shocked and lost for words. I managed to say, "Madam, I am sorry that this is how you perceive the issue I have raised. For me, when you said you would help me and be a key ally in my work, I candidly opened up to you. I thought I could confide in you so that you are aware of the reports out there." I went on to tell her that these were allegations, of course, but we had to go ahead and do some investigations to establish the truth.

Before I left she said, "Okay, Matembe, I will also carry out my own investigations to find out if Salim Saleh is involved in the UCB sale scandal." She promised to call and tell me what she would find out.

Although she never called to tell me what came out of her own investigation, within two weeks after our meeting, it came to light that Salim Saleh was irregularly involved in the buying and selling of UCB, which caused a big loss to the country.

Also, Hon Sam Kutesa was later to be censured by Parliament over corruption, while the good Hon Rukikaire resigned his ministerial position over the sale of UCB. It is now widely known that Hon Rukikaire was not corrupt and was only culpable for failing in his oversight role as Minister for Privatisation to detect the fraudulent deals that went on. As a matter of fact, when it was finally revealed that the UCB scandal involved Salim Saleh and the late Sulaiman Kiggundu, Hon Rukikaire came to see me in my office to seek my guidance as the Minister for Ethics and Integrity as to what he should do. He confided in me that he didn't know that there was fraudulence in the sale of UCB or even that Saleh was involved.

I advised him to resign since it was the most honourable thing to do in those circumstances, because the MPs were ready to censure him anyway. He wondered if resignation would not imply that he was guilty. I told him to make a statement telling the country what exactly happened, and to also apologize for the mess in his ministry, and own up to his falling short in the supervision of his ministry to the extent that serious business like the sale of UCB went on without his full involvement and awareness of all the details.

After our meeting, Hon Rukikaire wrote his statement and delivered it to Parliament. Up to now, he can stand in public with his head held high because he was exonerated from corruption.

It is also important to mention now that even when the allegation for which the First Lady had wrongly accused me of being involved in-petty Bahima-Bairu issues – turned out to be true, she did not at any one time call me to say that I was right.

From that time, my steady relationship with the

First Lady was derailed. The frequency of our meetings reduced, although, once in a while, she would call me to discuss one issue or another. In one of those meetings, I mentioned Gen Saleh's involvement in several corruption scandals at that time. This time she agreed with me and actually asked me to let her know whenever I heard anything about Saleh being involved in corruption deals, so that she could try and deter him from proceeding with the deals. Later, in fact, she told me that whenever she confronted Saleh after my tip-off, he would not deny the issue, but wondered where she got all the intelligence from. Of course, Saleh had no idea that it was I who was tipping off the First Lady. To this extent, she tried to support my anti-corruption efforts, as she had earlier promised.

When she eventually realized that the allegations I had made at the beginning were true, she changed her attitude towards me and our relationship went back to normal, although it was not as vibrant as before. However, I kept her abreast by telling her what the public was saying on these issues. Sometimes, her own name came up in the corruption talks, and whenever that happened, I would go and tell her. She always assured me that it was all false and that people were simply telling lies about her, and then we would get scriptures to read and pray about the false accusations.

We continued working together until the elections of 2001, in which people close to her and the First Family sponsored Ms Jovia Rwakishumba to run against me, as detailed in earlier chapters. Unfortunately, as Hon Sam Kutesa told me at that dinner, it was indeed true that the

First Lady was affected by my alleged support for Hon Winnie Byanyima which the newspaper swearing-in photo had falsely implied. Consequently, our meetings and friendship ground to a halt.

It was not until 2003, two years later,that I heard from the First Lady. Hon Mary Karooro Okurut, who was then the Press Secretary in the Office of the President, called me and told me that the First Lady wanted to see me. I was in Mbarara but I promised to contact her once I returned to Kampala. I went to her office and was informed that indeed she wanted to see me, but she was now engaged in some activities and would call me soon.

I kept waiting for her call which never came. At about that time, there was a women's prayer breakfast at Sheraton Hotel that I attended, and the First Lady was the guest of honour. After the function, she rushed out. As I was getting out of the hotel, she had already entered her car, but looking out of her window she saw me and motioned me to go to her.

When I reached the car, she greeted me but I was astonished by what she told me. *"Mbwenu Miria nkakwanga, nakwanga, nakwangira kimwe, kwonka Ruhanga yayanga, yaguma ayangire, nambwenu ninyija kukweta tubigambeho."* Meaning, I hated you and hated you, but the Lord did not like this; the Lord has been convicting me all this time and so I will call you and we shall talk.

I replied that all along I knew the devil had been fighting us, but I had been praying about it.

Somehow though, we never got to discuss the cause

of the hatred, but our relationship got back on track and she resumed delegating me to represent her in work that involved women.

In the meantime, I anxiously waited for the opportune time that the First Lady and I could discuss the cause of her hatred, but before that time came, the infamous Kyankwanzi 'third term' conference took place. As already discussed, I did not mince my words as I expressed my opposition to the removal of the presidential term limit, and I went as far as mobilising the country to resist the desecration of our constitution for the sake of her husband's continued stay in power. That effectively marked the end of my relationship with the First Lady.

# Chapter Twelve

## Embracing Life Outside Elective Politics and a Life-Long Commitment to the Women's Cause

### Life as a Backbencher in Parliament, Again

In the previous chapters, I have already mentioned how I and my colleagues, who were against the removal of the presidential term limit, were summarily dropped from President Museveni's cabinet, while those who promoted the 'third term' were generously rewarded with positions in the new cabinet. I went back to the backbench in Parliament where I was warmly embraced and re-elected Vice Chairperson of the Rules, Discipline and Privileges Committee and also became a member of the Parliamentary and Legal Affairs Committee.

In December, 2003, I was also elected as one of five members to represent Uganda in the inaugural Pan-African Parliament. At the Pan-African Parliament, I was elected the Chairperson of the Rules, Discipline and Privileges Committee where I was charged with the formulation of the Rules of Procedure that govern the Pan-African Parliament.

When the national elections came around again in 2006, I had not wanted to contest for my parliamentary seat again. As a Christian, I usually pray and ask God to guide me to make the best decisions. However, on this occasion I had not even asked God what to do. One of the reasons why I was not going to stand again was my pride. I did not know how to take defeat. I was convinced that as much as the support and love from my constituents was unwavering, it would not be translated into a win because President Museveni would unleash all the state machinery against me to ensure that I do not return to Parliament, since I was now his 'enemy'. Already, state-inspired violence had been meted out to Hon Winnie Byanyima and Mr James Garuga Musinguzi, and many others opposed to the President in the 2001 presidential elections, and therefore I could foresee the same being unleashed on me and my supporters. Besides the violence, I had a premonition that I would, at all costs, be rigged out.

The 2006 elections were to be the first multiparty elections in Uganda since 1980. I had not joined any political party, mainly because the sense of betrayal I had experienced under Museveni was still too fresh and heavy in my heart for me to trust any other leader. When finally the Lord prevailed upon me to contest, I hit the campaign trail as an independent candidate who was not affiliated to any political party. My message to the people was that I had come as an independent candidate to be their voice in Parliament. At the same time, I told the electorate that in case I was not voted into Parliament, my life would not stop. I had my skills and I could go on to other things.

To my great surprise, the campaigns were so smooth and there was no violence at all. Nobody attacked me or even harassed my supporters. As usual, the people in my district were excited to see that I had gone back to seek their vote. I never used money to bribe anyone but the people were genuinely attending my rallies in droves. In fact, my opponent was so intimidated that she never addressed any rallies on her own. She resorted to campaigning only at the group rallies which all NRM candidates would address, and her only message was that: "Matembe is no longer with us in the Movement, so please don't vote her."

At the end of it all, I can assure you that although I never petitioned court to contest the election results, I was thoroughly rigged out to the extent that I was declared a loser before the end of the counting of the votes. I remember women crying and wondering how all the votes they had cast for me could not translate into a victory.

## Life as a "Former"

On the 25th of February 2006, I, Miria Matembe, who had been a very important person (VIP) in the politics of Uganda, faced an overnight transformation. All of a sudden, I became a 'former' - 'Former Minister', 'Former MP', and 'Former Member of the Pan-African Parliament' because one is a member of the Pan-African Parliament only as long as they are a Member of an African national parliament. However, as my term in Parliament was to end in May, I was still going to be a serving MP until the end of May, 2006.

Shortly after the elections, I received excellent news: my application for The Reagan-Fascell Democracy Fellowship had been accepted. I had applied for the scholary fellowship during the time when I had not intended to contest for Parliament again. God always has a perfect plan for me and His goodness never stops to amaze me.

On 6th March, 2006 I landed in Washington, DC, for the five-month Reagan-Fascell Democracy Fellowship provided by the United States National Endowment for Democracy (NED). What a safe landing! I had a nice flat to live in and I received a handsome stipend of USD 25,000. So by the time Kampala was busy with the handover and swearing-in of a new government, I was safely in my Washington nook pursuing the Fellowship program. God gave me a soft landing not only to pursue the scholarly program but also to relax, meditate, contemplate and profoundly reflect on my life to find what I needed to do next.

While in Washington, I pondered deeply about God's purpose for me – what my dream in life really was. Without a doubt, my dream was and still is fighting for gender equality and women empowerment and in a broader sense fighting for justice and fairness for all people. I acknowledged that over the past years, politics and the parliament had been the vehicle to push my cause, but now that I was out of politics, what next?

I resolved that I could still effectively pursue my dream outside parliament. I remembered the words of John Maxwell, that: "A great leader's courage to fulfill his or her vision comes from passion not position." After all, before I joined parliament I had been a founder member of many NGOs and an active participant and activist in the civil society in Uganda. I decided that I would use my experience of 17 years in parliament to set up an organisation that would help women to overcome some of the challenges women leaders in the political arena were facing; and, particularly the constraints that many women leaders, including myself, had to grapple with from day to day. It would be an organisation that would empower women leaders to effectively participate and influence the governance agenda.

While it is true that the inclusion of women at all levels of government leadership had grown due to deliberate government policies like affirmative action and the principle of gender balance, this proliferation of women in the local councils, parliament and other constitutional bodies was not translating into effective lobbying and improvement of the plight of women in Uganda. The women's voice was neither loud nor effective enough to influence the governance agenda to make it responsive to the interests and the needs of the women of Uganda.

Consequently, many women took advantage of affirmative action to contest for the leadership positions available for women not out of any conviction or passion for the women empowerment cause, but as a job opportunity. Having realised this gap during my stay in Washington, I developed the idea to establish an organisation whose purpose would be to build a cadre of women with skills, knowledge and an all-round capacity to participate in politics with a vision. I had come to realise that just as political parties deliberately identify, recruit, groom, empower and mentor leaders, it was also necessary for women's organisations to deliberately set out to identify, interest, train and empower women to participate meaningfully and effectively in politics and governance. My conviction was that the organisation that I would form would enable us to create a pool of women who would be ready to contest in elections, not as a way to secure a job, as was happening, but with a mission to influence the governance agenda for equality and women's empowerment.

Also, I wanted to deal with the problem of women being co-opted into state structures, as I explained in Chapter Ten. Many politically active women got swallowed by state structures and consequently were unable to influence those structures to make them responsive to women's needs. At the same time, the women were denied the opportunity to speak from outside these state structures to challenge the State. At one time in Uganda, we had a strong women's movement that could challenge the State from outside , but now the women's movement was weak and the women within the State structures had been swallowed up. Thus the voice of the women in Uganda was dying.

In light of the above, I wrote a project paper for establishment of a centre for women in governance. The National Endowment for Democracy liked the idea and promised to give us seed money for the organisation. True to their word, when I returned to Uganda in August 2006, National Endowment for Democracy provided me with the funds and that marked the birth of Centre for Women in Governance (CEWIGO). CEWIGO is now a fully-fledged civil society organisation that runs independently from me as the founder.

All through my time in Washington, I had asked myself what would become of me when I returned to Uganda. I spent a lot of time praying and asking God to show me the way. I landed on scripture verses that resonated with my life then, particularly the story of Prophet Elijah. After he had declared that there would be no rain in Israel for three years, God took him to a brook where he was provided for by a raven which brought him meat. He survived on the meat and water from the brook while the rest of Israel suffered in the severe drought. When the brook dried up, God told Prophet Elijah to go to Zarephath where he would find a widow who would look after him.

Like Elijah, I looked at my life in Washington as someone at the brook being provided for by a raven. But as the Fellowship came to a close, I prayed to God to provide 'a widow' who would meet my needs when I returned to Uganda. It is important to note here that in Uganda, even as an MP or a minister, as long as you are not corrupt, you do not become wealthy. So I had no money that would help me start up again. The little savings I had got from the Parliament saving scheme had been spent during my last campaign. Therefore, one can understand the basis of my insecurity.

I returned to Uganda in August 2006 on the basis of that prayer. Like Naomi in the Bible, who went to a faraway land with her husband and two sons to look for greener pastures, but returned distressed and empty-handed, with only herself and her widowed daughter-in-law, I too had left the country as a powerful Honourable Member of Parliament of Uganda and the Pan-African Parliament, but here I was, landing at Entebbe Airport as a simple ordinary citizen.

After seventeen years of glamour and limelight, I sat in my living room and felt lost. I didn't know what to do when I got out of the house; didn't know how I would face people. I worried about how people would perceive me. It felt as if I was a thief or a wrongdoer of sorts! I felt rejected and abandoned. I don't believe this was something that was unique to me, but rather a situation that befalls many ex-leaders on the continent.

In Africa, the moment you fall out with the establishment, despite your long, distinguished career of service to the nation, it appears as if you lose everything – no honour or respect. Nothing. You are treated like trash. In fact, it has been an old method of authoritarian rulers in Africa to subdue opponents and dissenters not only by using outright brute force and violence, but also the destruction of the dissenter's economic base, the demonisation of his or her character, disenfranchisement and even dehumanisation. After my experience, I figured out why some leaders in Africa continue serving governments they no longer believe in; it is because of the fear of the unknown once they leave office.

Ironically, although I didn't have a regular source of income, my main fear was not about how to survive in terms of provisions and money. What sent chills down my spine was the fear of disappearing into oblivion. I was accustomed to being a respected public figure who got frequent invitations to speak at conferences, cocktails and other gatherings because of the positions I had held. So what next, now that I was just a 'former,' I wondered.

In the meantime, I kept reminding God about the widow of Zarephath. I implored God to quickly provide my 'widow of Zarephath' who would care for me and my family.

My friends tried to comfort and strengthen me by saying that all would be well. One suggested that I could find a small office to rent in town. Another one suggested that I could go downtown to the slums of Katwe and find cheap furniture for the office. I told them there was no way I was going to Katwe. "When God has favoured you, He raises you from one level to another, and He never lowers you, so He cannot take me back to Katwe," I said. We shared the joke and simply laughed it off, but deep inside me, the fear and anxiety were still much alive.

While contemplating the serious situation and meditating in my room one day, I heard God's unmistakable voice. He told me that I would never disappear into oblivion. He said that if I thought that the jobs and positions I held were the ones putting me in the limelight, I was mistaken. He said to me, "I am the one who has brought you this far, and although the jobs and positions are gone, I have not abandoned you. I am still with you. You are mine and you will never disappear into oblivion." I gave a sigh of relief. I relaxed because my God had assured me that He would not forsake me.

Meanwhile, I started drafting the constitution for CEWIGO. I mobilised a team of eminent women: Dr Maxine Ankrah of the Ankrah Foundation and other colleagues with whom we had co-founded ACFODE; Hon Sarah Kiyingi Kyama, with whom I had been thrown out of cabinet for opposing the lifting of the presidential term limit; and Ms Maude Mugisha, who had been the pioneer Executive Secretary of ACFODE and with whom I had worked closely for four years when I was the chairperson of ACFODE in its peak days. I shared with them my vision of establishing CEWIGO and they bought the idea. They agreed to help me establish it. With their go ahead, I continued to work on the necessary documents. It was during that period when the Lord assured me that He would never let me disappear into oblivion. The Lord's assurance gave me confidence and vigour to work even harder.

True to His word of assurance, the Lord has kept us

aloft. I can assure you that to date, I have not disappeared into oblivion – whether in Uganda or abroad. At the time of writing this book, more than ten years out of official public service, I can assure you that I have achieved more than I ever did before. Glory to God!

As I now had more time on my hands than before, it became a custom for me to take a walk around Port Bell area every morning as a form of exercise. One morning as I walked, I reminded God about my 'widow'. To be honest, I didn't even know whether I meant a physical widow or what exactly. Then I heard a voice saying, "You mean you have not seen her?"

I turned around and asked, "Where is she?"

"Aren't you eating? Don't you drive your own vehicle? Don't you have fuel? Don't you have airtime? Don't you have everything you need"

Suddenly, it occurred to me that the 'widow of Zarephath' meant provision, and since I didn't lack anything, it meant that the "widow" was already with me, caring for my every need. I came home and told my husband that I had met God. I told him everything – I was now dependent on my God who was providing for my every need. Up till now, I can still vividly recall that spot on the road where the Lord answered me. I can only compare it with that place where Jacob met with the angel of the Lord who wrestled with him (*Genesis 32: 22-31, New International Version*).

When I reached that exact same spot the next morning, the Spirit of the Lord told me that, "Remember the widow of Zarephath had to part with some flour and oil to bake a cake for the man of God." To me, that meant that even though I had a little provision, I had to take some of it to God. The next day, I got some money *(the Lord had told me the amount),* went to All Saints Church, Nakasero, and handed it over to a priest, telling him that I was planting a seed so that the Word of God would germinate and flourish. Since then, I have never lacked for anything, in the same way that the flour and oil of the widow of Zarephath never ran out until the rains came.

## Resisting the Call to Join Elective Politics Again

Many of my supporters from both Mbarara, my district of birth, and Bushenyi, my husband's district, which has therefore become my district also, have from time to time implored me to make a comeback into national politics to represent them in Parliament. I have always maintained, however, that I played my role in parliamentary politics and finished it. I will not stand for parliamentary elections again. But whence cometh this resolve and strong conviction?

Once again, one day while I was at home praying, the Lord led me to the scripture John 21:1–9. In this particular scripture that talks about Jesus' resurrection, but before His ascension to heaven, His apostles had spent some time without seeing him. They were uncertain and felt that Jesus had abandoned them. They became quite desperate. Peter invited his fellow disciples to go fishing with him. They agreed, but after fishing the whole night, they hadn't caught any fish. As they were cleaning their nets after their unproductive night's venture, they saw a man standing on the shore. He asked whether they had made any catch, and when they said no, He told them to cast their nets on the *right* side of the boat. Amazingly, they caught a lot of fish, meaning that they had been fishing on the *wrong* side. Upon that miracle, they realized that the man was Jesus, their Lord and Master. He asked them to come with some of their catch to the shore for breakfast. The story tells us that when they got to the shore, they found that Jesus was already roasting fish for them *(John 21: 1-14, New International Version)*. Upon meditating on this Bible story, the Lord revealed to me three clear and distinct lessons that have helped to sustain me:

The first message is that I am not supposed to go back from where the Lord called me. Remember, Jesus had told the disciples that He would make them fishers of men not fishermen, which is what they had been doing. Thus, when they went back to fish, they could not get any fish. The anointing for that calling was over. This meant to me that I could not go back to contest for parliamentary elections. My anointing to serve in that capacity was over. Rather, I was to await my new assignment with its appropriate anointing.

The second lesson is this. When you find yourself in a difficult situation, and you are anxious that you are lost, do not despair. When you don't see God and fear that you're alone, do not lose hope. He is there with you. He knows what is going on and continues to watch over you whether you see Him or not. The disciples thought they were alone with no master and so had gone out to fend for themselves. However, we see that Jesus had never left them and, in fact, appeared to them exactly where they were. This shows that He knows where we are all the time, whether we see Him or not.

The third lesson is that God does not only know where we are and watch over us, but He has already prepared for us what to eat, what to drink and all that. When the disciples came to the shore, they found that Jesus had already started roasting fish for them. Therefore, I knew that God has already prepared for me what to do, where to do it and when to do it – including all my provisions. It is He who will break my fast. It is He who will give me a deployment.

On one occasion, when Bushenyi Municipality was carved out as an electoral constituency, some people from Bushenyi called me and earnestly asked me to go and contest on their behalf. Just as I was thinking the request over, I got a call to go to South Sudan for a consultancy. To me, this meant that God had brought the South Sudan opportunity as a reminder that I should not go back into parliamentary politics. When the same constituency held a bye-election, another supporter called me on the day of nomination to ask me to contest. Once again, I was not available as I was in South Africa. This again meant that God clearly did not want me back into parliamentary politics. I am therefore patiently waiting on God as He weaves the grand design for my destiny as He has promised me.

## My Mandate in Life

As I have said throughout this book, my lifelong struggle has been to fight for gender equality, women's empowerment, justice and fairness. This is what drives me. I went into politics to get a platform from which to espouse the cause. So, even though I no longer have that political platform, the dream in me is still alive.

I remember one special moment when I felt that God had clearly endorsed and blessed my work with women. This was after the Kyankwanzi debate on lifting the term limits to extend President Museveni's rule, where I stood up and vehemently opposed that plan and the President bashed and humiliated me. I was so incensed and angry that when I went into my room that night, I was determined to resign my cabinet position. I prayed to God for guidance on what to do.

In the morning, God answered me through a scripture that clearly gave me my mandate in life: Isaiah 49, particularly verses 2 and 3 - *He made my mouth like a sharpened sword, in the shadow of his hand he hid me; he made me into a polished arrow and concealed me in his quiver. He said to me, "You are my servant, Israel (Miria), in whom I will display my splendor."*

Through that scripture, the Lord also told me that Uganda was too small for me. He would make me a light unto other nations. That scripture clearly spelt out that my mandate was to use my mouth to speak out for the cause without fear or favour for I would be under the coverage and protection of God. My mandate had been expanded to other nations, and as such, God opened doors for me to go and train and mentor women across the world in political participation. I have been to Lesotho, Sierra Leone, Bangladesh, Kenya, Zambia, South Africa, Sudan, South Sudan, Nigeria, Botswana, to mention but a few. I have been mostly engaged by international organisations such as UNDP, NDI, and ISIS-WICCE, and at other times, I have been contracted directly by local women's organisations and government. Through these programs, many women who had previously not been interested in joining politics picked up an interest, while those who were already in politics found new purpose. The testimonies from countries like Sierra Leone about how enriching the programs I have participated in have been are really humbling for me.

As it says in Isaiah 54, God enlarged my tents (boundaries) because He had a new purpose for me. He wanted me to have an impact on women beyond Uganda; who was I not to heed to His call? On a few occasions where I tried to resist His call, He always gently pushed me back in line. One such incident was what happened just after I had established CEWIGO. After the National Endowment for Democracy fulfilled their pledge of giving me seed money, I put word out to other funders. Soon, DANIDA and the Ford Foundation followed suit. Armed with all this funding and support, I got an office, furnished it fully and was ready to swing into action.

However, when I went to pray and dedicate the office, God told me that this was not the dream and assignment

He had for me. I pleaded and negotiated with Him that when work outside Uganda coincided with in-country work, I would always give priority to the former. So I stayed at CEWIGO, but within the first week, the Pan-African Parliament in South Africa called me to do some consultancy work.

Just after returning from South Africa, I got another call to go to Vancouver. That is when I was awarded an Honorary Doctorate of Laws by Victoria University in Canada. Therefore, as you can see, the Lord made sure that I was busy and more engaged outside Uganda than inside.

In another instance, I had planned to have a workshop in Gulu, but about three days to the Gulu workshop, I got a call from Spain to go to Nigeria. I was really determined to go to Gulu, but when I prayed, again it became clear that the will of God was for me to head to Nigeria. I searched around for a replacement to conduct the Gulu workshop and off to Nigeria I went.

At around that time, UMEME, the electricity supplier had billed me an exorbitant electricity amount which I believe was concocted. I believe this was another of those evil tactics that the government uses to embarrass and publicly humiliate political opponents. After the two days' work in Nigeria, however, I was paid enough Euros and this enabled me to settle the electricity bill. Can you imagine that! It was then that I realized that the Lord really was present in my affairs. He had stopped me from going to Gulu and guided me to Nigeria where I would find my provision that would help me with the outstanding electricity bill.

On my return, as usual, I sought God's guidance and He led me to Isaiah 48: 1-12 which talks about stubborn Israel. From that day, I decided that I would not continue my personal involvement in CEWIGO. I handed it over to someone else to run. I am happy to say that it is still running, flourishing, inspiring and empowering women in governance, without relying on me as the founder.

## Conclusion

I have always told people that for me, it is not the position that makes me. On the contrary, I make the position count because of my personal attributes and commitment that I bring to the position. It has been more than twelve years since I last held any official position, but my star and authority have not dimmed or dwindled at all. I still wield similar authority that I had as a cabinet minister and MP. When I walk into a police station or meet policemen on the road, they stop to salute me.

Indeed, I still use every platform and every opportunity I get to promote women's issues; if there is any topical issue to be addressed, the press cannot rest until they hear my views; they even come to me in my home. This is because I am serving my purpose. The secret to success, I believe, is knowing who you are in God, trusting and believing in Him, and identifying His purpose for your life and pursuing it. When you know who you are in God, you do not undermine yourself, you do not underrate yourself; rather, you draw your confidence from Him who says that: "I will never leave you, nor forsake you".

In 1996, before I was appointed Minister for Ethics and Integrity, President Museveni called me to give me a job. He wanted to appoint me as a Director of one of the intelligence organisations. He told me that they were stealing money and he wanted someone with integrity to help him protect the money. I turned his request down and told him that with all due respect, I could not take that job because that was not where my interest lay; that I did not think it was God's purpose for my life. Unfortunately, there are many people who simply take on jobs because they've been invited to take them, whether or not it is God's purpose for their lives.

From my early days of activism, I set out to use my life as an example to all. I am proud to say that I have lived my life in a way that epitomises the fact that it is possible for a woman to fight valiantly for a cause she believes in, a cause that is bigger than herself and her family, without jeopardising her family and without neglecting her domestic and reproductive responsibilities: the responsibilities of a wife and mother.

Despite the furore that surrounds the name Matembe, I am just an ordinary woman with an extraordinary dream. It is a delicate balance. By the grace of God I have been happily married for forty three years now. I have also been able to bring up four biological children, sons; and they are now all responsible young men. Three of them have already secured for me daughters-in-love. I have also raised nephews and nieces, one of whom has given me a son-in-love and twin grandchildren. I do not credit myself; I give the credit to God.

I am also thankful to God for giving me a gracious husband. I think my husband is the best of husbands because he is the one I got. But the most important gift that my husband gave me is that of not interfering with my freedom. He is not averse to my politicking and to my frequent travels, both locally and internationally.

One of the reasons why some women in Parliament, cabinet and in other political positions have broken marriages is that when they get into public life they go wild, engage in immoral affairs, or otherwise misbehave and stop respecting their husbands. In fact, many people who see where I am and who I am say: "This Matembe (my husband) must be suffering; we really do not know how he manages that woman." I tell such people that I am not a factory, or a project, or an office to be managed. A woman is a human being who needs love and understanding. My husband gives that to me and I fully respect him for this.

My message to anyone out there who looks up to me is simple: do not just jump into anything, jump into politics, jump into leadership, jump into whatever. Each one of us has a God-given purpose to serve, and must do it in their generation. Identify God's purpose for you, align yourself to it, and you will succeed.

I have learnt that life does not exist in positions or possessions, but it exists in knowing God's purpose for your life and serving it; rendering a service to God's people in such a way that gives Him glory. Positions and possessions are given to us by God to facilitate us to serve His purpose. Each one of us was given talents according to our ability, and when we use these talents according to God's will, we shall be rewarded. I believe that one day I shall receive the commendation that is written in Mathew 25:23: *"Well done good and faithful servant... come and share your master's happiness."*

As for my poor country Uganda, I have watched the democratic path dwindling further and further, to the extent that we cannot talk about the principle of separation of power anymore. I am completing the writing of this book after the most irregularly conducted elections of 2016, as declared by both the national and international election observers – an opinion shared by many Ugandans. The elections were characterised by violence, harassment and intimidation of members of the opposition, voter bribery and disenfranchisement of voters through poor management of the whole electoral process.

After being sworn in as President for his new term, having ruled the country for 30 years, President Museveni began by prevailing on the 10th Parliament to vote the Speaker and Deputy Speaker of his choice. Parliamentarians from the ruling NRM party, as has been the case in recent years, were bribed. Still not certain that they would vote as per the inducement, he uncharacteristically pitched camp in the Parliament's chamber to personally see to it that the MPs voted as instructed. Without any remorse or shame, he thereafter addressed Parliament and expressed his pleasure that the 10th Parliament had passed its first test. But which test? The test of surrendering its powers and authority to the Executive? What a pity!

As things stand now, the situation is likely to get worse because President Museveni has shed off all pretense of niceties and its now brute force at work. At the height of the removal of age limit debate dubbed *Togikwatako*, the opposition MPs put up a spirited fight in parliament to defend the sanctity of the constitution. The regime was not having any of it and on 27th September, 2017 a gang (believed to be members of the elite presidential guard) invaded the house and beat up MPs leaving some of them hospitalised and others like Hon Betty Nambooze with permanent disabilities. Unfortunately, Museveni eventually got his way and the age limit was scrapped by Parliament.

Clearly, there is an urgent need for transformative leadership in Uganda; from the current one that is self-centred and power-oriented to a people-centred and service-oriented leadership. Yet what I see now is consolidation of dictatorship, state capture and total militarisation and life presidency. Cry my beloved country.

Ugandans, like the biblical children of Israel, continue to wander around the mountain in the desert rather than cross to the Promised Land. What a pity for the lost opportunity. Surely, Ugandans need to hear a loud voice from God telling us that we have been on this mountain long enough and it is time to break camp and move on.

**New Vis**

# I will remind Museveni to retire, says Matembe

**By A. G. Musamali**

ETHICS and integrity state minister Miria Matembe, on Monday said she will oppose President Museveni if he seeks another term of office.

"If Museveni does not remember to retire in 2006 I will remind him,"

Matembe said.

She was opening the Isis-Women's International Cross Cultural Exchange regional training programme at Hotel Equatoria.

The two weeks training programme has attracted 28 women activists from several African nations.

GO ON: Matembe accompanies Byanyima to be sworn in

## Matembe, Tumwine clash

## Matembe, Tumwine clash over 'Movt' bus

**By Felix Basiim**
In Mbarara
**& Alex B. Atuhaire**
in Kampala

The minister of Ethics and Integrity, Miria Matembe, seeking re-election for the Mbarara women parliamentary seat, clashed with Maj. Gen Elly Tumwine in Mbarara town yesterday.

Matembe confronted Tumwine at Mbarara High Street following a mobilisation campaign by the famous Movement "yellow bus" which was heading to Kashaari to drum up support for Nathan Mutwengua who is standing against Maj John Kazoora.

Matembe and Tumwine reportedly exchanged hot words.

Made in the USA
Middletown, DE
14 October 2023

40773740R00163